Dr. C. M. Wormington

First, Second, and Third John

INTERPRETATION
A Bible Commentary for Teaching and Preaching

INTERPRETATION

A BIBLE COMMENTARY FOR TEACHING AND PREACHING

James Luther Mays, *Editor*
Patrick D. Miller, Jr., *Old Testament Editor*
Paul J. Achtemeier, *New Testament Editor*

D. MOODY SMITH

First, Second, and Third John

INTERPRETATION

A Bible Commentary
for Teaching and Preaching

John Knox Press
LOUISVILLE

Library of Congress Cataloging-in-Publication Data

Smith, D. Moody (Dwight Moody)
   First, Second, and Third John / D. Moody Smith.
      p.   cm. — (Interpretation, a Bible commentary for
teaching and preaching)
   Includes bibliographical references.
   ISBN 0-8042-3147-8

   1. Bible. N.T. Epistles of John—Commentaries.   2. Bible. N.T.
Epistles of John—Homiletical use.   I. Title.   II. Series.
BS2805.3.S65 1991
227'.9407—dc20   91-3484

© 1991 John Knox Press
10 9 8 7 6 5 4 3 2
Printed in the United States of America

SERIES PREFACE

This series of commentaries offers an interpretation of the books of the Bible. It is designed to meet the need of students, teachers, ministers, and priests for a contemporary expository commentary. These volumes will not replace the historical critical commentary or homiletical aids to preaching. The purpose of this series is rather to provide a third kind of resource, a commentary which presents the integrated result of historical and theological work with the biblical text.

An interpretation in the full sense of the term involves a text, an interpreter, and someone for whom the interpretation is made. Here, the text is what stands written in the Bible in its full identity as literature from the time of "the prophets and apostles," the literature which is read to inform, inspire, and guide the life of faith. The interpreters are scholars who seek to create an interpretation which is both faithful to the text and useful to the church. The series is written for those who teach, preach, and study the Bible in the community of faith.

The comment generally takes the form of expository essays. It is planned and written in the light of the needs and questions which arise in the use of the Bible as Holy Scripture. The insights and results of contemporary scholarly research are used for the sake of the exposition. The commentators write as exegetes and theologians. The task which they undertake is both to deal with what the texts say and to discern their meaning for faith and life. The exposition is the unified work of one interpreter.

The text on which the comment is based is the Revised Standard Version of the Bible and, since its appearance, the New Revised Standard Version. The general availability of these translations makes the printing of a text in the commentary unnecessary. The commentators have also had other current versions in view as they worked and refer to their readings where it is helpful. The text is divided into sections appropriate to the particular book; comment deals with passages as a whole, rather than proceeding word by word, or verse by verse.

Writers have planned their volumes in light of the requirements set by the exposition of the book assigned to them. Biblical books differ in character, content, and arrangement. They also differ in the way they have been and are used in the liturgy, thought, and devotion of the church. The distinctiveness and use of particular books have been taken into account in decisions about the approach, emphasis, and use of space in the commentaries. The goal has been to allow writers to develop the format which provides for the best presentation of their interpretation.

The result, writers and editors hope, is a commentary which both explains and applies, an interpretation which deals with both the meaning and the significance of biblical texts. Each commentary reflects, of course, the writer's own approach and perception of the church and world. It could and should not be otherwise. Every interpretation of any kind is individual in that sense; it is one reading of the text. But all who work at the interpretation of scripture in the church need the help and stimulation of a colleague's reading and understanding of the text. If these volumes serve and encourage interpretation in that way, their preparation and publication will realize their purpose.

The Editors

PREFACE

The Gospel of John never suffers from lack of attention. The invitation to write this commentary, however, caused me to pay more serious attention to the letters in a course on the Gospel and Epistles of John, which I have taught for many years. Heretofore, I had concentrated on the Gospel, pleading reasons of time and maintaining that whoever had mastered the Gospel would have no difficulty with the letters. Teaching the letters has, however, taught me that while the Gospel is important for understanding them, it by no means renders them redundant or superfluous. The letters obviously address a different audience or setting, and somewhat different issues. These issues continue to merit the attention of the church in its theology, ethics, and praxis.

The dedication of this book to Raymond E. Brown is a small token of the debt that all who study the Gospel and Epistles of John owe him. His commentaries are benchmarks not only of scholarship but of the increasingly ecumenical character of the exegetical enterprise as it has developed during his career. He has contributed enormously in both areas. I do not imagine that he will approve everything in this relatively slim commentary, but trust that he will discern how his own work has importantly influenced mine, even where I do not find myself in complete agreement with him.

I was able to revise this commentary and bring it to completion during a term spent at the Center of Theological Inquiry in Princeton, New Jersey. The founders of the Center, particularly the late Dr. James I. McCord, understood the importance of providing such auspices for theological research and writing. I thank the trustees of the Center for inviting me to become a member. My thanks also to the secretarial staff of Duke Divinity School, especially Ms. Sarah Freedman and Mrs. Gail Chappell, who deciphered and reproduced the marks I made with my pocket word processor. I am grateful to my graduate assistant Craig Keener for his careful reading and correction of the manuscript, as well as for his criticism and helpful suggestions. Needless to say, the editors, Professors Paul J. Achtemeier and James L. Mays, also offered me valuable criticism and counsel from the beginning. I owe them thanks for that, as well as for their invitation to write the commentary and for their patiently prodding me to finish it.

D.M.S.

November, 1990

CONTENTS

3

To
Raymond E. Brown, S.S.,
who has taught us so much about the Gospel
and Epistles of John

Introduction

The Johannine Epistles* offer an unusual challenge and
reward to the interpreter. Although they pose some difficult
exegetical and historical problems, their theological and ethical
message is profound and important. Commenting on 1 John,
Martin Luther rendered a judgment that is both eloquent and
true: "This is an outstanding Epistle. It can buoy up afflicted
hearts. Furthermore, it has John's style and manner of expression, so beautifully and gently does it picture Christ to us." With
good reason, modern critical studies have often presented the
Gospel and Epistles of John as the capstone of the development
of theological and ethical thought within the New Testament.
To reach theological heights through a simple language and
style is the distinctive hallmark and accomplishment of these
writings.

Yet accurate or precise understanding of the Johannine
letters often eludes a first or casual reading. Simple as they may
seem, they are not without ambiguity and obscurity, for they
were written long ago to situations familiar to author and readers but not obvious to us. Much that they shared and could
assume was left unsaid. Thus careful and thoughtful reading is
necessary to unlock and grasp fully the theological and ethical
treasure they contain. Just the interplay of profound theological
and ethical truth with quite concrete and difficult circumstances of individual and church life is a part of the genius of
the letters and warrants careful attention to the settings and
problems to which they are addressed.

These letters invite us to a journey of discovery, from the
well known and familiar to the less familiar but nevertheless

---

*"Epistle" is the traditional term. We shall more often use the modern
term "letter," which is employed in the RSV titles. Although in modern
scholarship a distinction has occasionally been made on the basis of the
difference between private communication (letter) and public (epistle), it does not correspond entirely to ancient usage and is probably
not useful.

rewarding. The terms, concepts, and expressions strike the reader, particularly the Christian reader, as familiar. They evoke elemental concepts such as life and light, but also distinctively Christian views of sin and the saving work of Christ. Yet exactly how the saving work of Christ is to be understood theologically, and what it calls for ethically, are matters of great importance that lay upon us the obligation to work and struggle in order to understand more precisely what is at stake. The Johannine letters themselves are the product of such work and struggle, and they summon us to become involved in the same task, which is the work of Christ's church in every generation. It is precisely the essence of the Christian revelation, however, that it does not begin afresh with every generation, but looks to its past, that is, ultimately, to its origin for its bearings. The author of our letters knows this very well and therefore invites his readers and, indeed, readers of any generation to turn with him to Jesus Christ, the one who has been seen and touched, to whom faithful witness has been borne and must be borne ever again.

The Nature of the Johannine Letters

The Johannine letters clearly belong to the same circle or school of early Christianity that produced the Gospel of John, which in turn has some points of similarity and affinity with the Revelation to John. Already in the third century Dionysius, bishop of Alexandria, pointed out the many similarities of style, language, and theology between the Gospel and letters and at the same time called attention to their differences from Revelation, concluding that while the Gospel and letters were the work of the Apostle, the Revelation to John could not be. This is a literary-critical judgment that has stood the test of time remarkably well.

In his *Explanatory Notes upon the New Testament*, John Wesley wrote: "The great similitude, or rather sameness, both of spirit and expression, which runs through John's Gospel and all his epistles is a clear evidence of their being written by the same person" (p. 902). Whether the same person actually wrote the Gospel and letters has now become a debated question, but modern scholars agree that the position of Dionysius is an intelligent one, based on important observations. In fact, W. G. Kümmel, in his standard *Introduction to the New Testament*,

8

pointedly refuses to endorse the view that the letters were written by someone other than the Fourth Evangelist (pp. 445, 450). The Revelation to John is another matter, as Dionysius clearly saw, and it is worth observing that even Wesley, who accepted it as apostolic, made no mention of the matter of its authorship in his introductory note.

The question of authorship is not, however, our primary concern, although we shall return to it later in this introduction. The first step in interpretation is to decide about the nature of the writings with which we are dealing. Wesley called 1 John an epistle or letter but promptly qualified that statement by referring to it as a tract, having doubtless observed that, unlike 2 and 3 John and the Pauline epistles, 1 John has no epistolary beginning or ending. There is no salutation; the author does not identify himself. In this respect 1 John differs even from 2 and 3 John, which are clearly cast in the form of letters. Yet 1 John is manifestly some kind of written communication or tract, for the author repeatedly refers to the fact that he is writing, not speaking (2:1, 7, 12, etc.). Thus there is good reason to stick with the traditional language of "epistles" or "letters" in discussing these writings. The problems of interpretation that apply to any of the New Testament letters apply to them as well.

Understanding and Interpreting the Johannine Letters

Reading and trying to understand a New Testament letter is somewhat like eavesdropping on a conversation of which we can overhear only one side, for we do not know what the addressees have said or thought except as we can infer it from the letter we possess. Sometimes it is not so important to know what the original readers had said or thought in order to understand the letter in question. For example, Paul's letter to the Romans can be read with genuine understanding and appreciation by any reader who pays attention to its content and argument and takes the trouble to find out what Paul's conceptuality and language would have conveyed to first-century readers. Some familiarity with the Christian theological tradition generally is also helpful, although it must be open to correction from one's reading and further study. Yet it is not of crucial importance—although it may be helpful—to know what the Roman Christians were doing, thinking, or saying in order to grasp Paul's arguments. More important is our understanding of Paul's own theological vocabulary and concepts, as well as his use of scripture and Jewish as well as Christian tradition.

On the other hand, in the case of a letter like 1 Corinthians the situation is much different. What Paul has to say is closely related to what had been going on in the church at Corinth. Oftentimes Paul helps us a great deal by describing the situation he is addressing. Thus, for example, he describes the divisions in the church, caused by the Corinthians' adhering to individual leaders, including Paul himself (1:10–17); or he specifies certain kinds of immorality (chaps. 5 and 6). He may discuss the relationship between men and women (chap. 7), a subject to which most of us can relate and about which some of us feel quite as competent as Paul to give advice. Yet even here there are puzzles, and some of Paul's advice may sound strange. Who is the betrothed woman or virgin (7:36–38), particularly in view of her male partner's option of either consummating the marriage or remaining celibate? Here is a situation to which there is no modern analogy. Similarly, the problem presented by eating meat offered to idols (chaps. 8 and 10) now has no counterpart in Western culture, although the theological and ethical points Paul makes still have relevance. The celebration of the Lord's Supper (11:17–34) is familiar enough to Christians, but the situation, or the social conventions, that have led to the problem Paul addresses are not. In order to understand exactly the thrust of what Paul is saying to this specific setting and problem, we cannot avoid completely an element of conjecture or hypothetical historical reconstruction. Yet Paul supplies us ample data, even though the Corinthians can speak to us only through him.

With the Johannine letters we have yet another state of affairs. None of them, not even 1 John, presents a sustained theological argument. Any effort to outline the structure of 1 John carries with it some element of uncertainty or inconclusiveness. The contrast with Romans in this respect is all too evident. Yet while there is no developed theological argument, quite obviously strong theological convictions or concerns are at work. Equally obvious is the fact that these convictions are clearly and pointedly set over against those of certain opponents (e.g., in 2:18–19; 4:1–3), but neither these opponents nor the exact nature of their offending views are named or described specifically. We may infer, however, that the opponents are not only doctrinally, but also morally, deficient and culpable (cf. 4:20). In 3 John a specific problem of church polity or jurisdiction comes into view as the author deplores the attitude and conduct of a certain Diotrephes (vv. 9–10). Presumably the author and Diotrephes are rival claimants to authority over this specific church and perhaps others, but even the character and basis for their claim of authority is unclear. Other examples suggesting specific situations could be adduced.

Unlike Paul, the author of these letters does not give us much concrete data to furnish handholds for interpretation. Thus while these brief letters do not stand on their own but apparently address specific situations, we do not know, and cannot define, these situations with a high degree of confidence. Wesley wrote that the author's expression "my beloved children" includes "the whole body of Christians" (p. 905), but we are no longer as certain as he was. On the one hand, we may wish to defend such a reading as appropriate to contemporary Christians. On the other, we have to allow for the distinct possibility that the author had a discrete group of believers in view, over whom he had authority and for whom he felt responsibility. (But again Kümmel, p. 437, agrees with Wesley that "the entirety of Christianity is being addressed.") When we read of the great, central themes of Christian theology and experience in the Johannine letters—sin, faith, forgiveness, love—we rightly sense that we know about what we are reading. Yet we lack a specific historical, and interpretative, context for them. We have, however, a literary context in which to put them, namely, the other Johannine writings, especially the Gospel of John; but how the letters relate to this context is itself problematic, and we shall have to deal with this set of problems.

Questions of Authorship

Did the Same Person Write the Gospel and Letters?

Within the Johannine context, there are good reasons for asking whether the same author wrote the Gospel and letters. There are real differences between them. First of all, there is apparently a difference in audience or setting.

The Gospel of John portrays Jesus in sharp conflict with people simply called "the Jews." Those who follow Jesus are said

11

to fear "the Jews" (John 20:19). They are afraid that if they openly avow their faith in him, "the Jews" will put them out of the synagogue (John 9:22; 12:42; cf. 16:2). Although mainly distinctly Christian issues and concerns are dealt with in Jesus' farewell discourses and prayer with his disciples (chaps. 13–17), the Gospel narrative is set against the backdrop of harsh hostility between Jesus' disciples and "the Jews." Exactly who these Jews are is never clearly stated. Certainly they are not to be identified with the whole Jewish people—not then, and much less now (cf. Sloyan, xiii–xiv). Probably they are to be equated with the oft-mentioned Pharisees, who represent the Pharisaic authorities of the latter part of the first century, with whom the Johannine Christians were in bitter conflict (cf. J. Louis Martyn, *History and Theology in the Fourth Gospel*).

In any event, Jews are not even mentioned in the letters, and the issues and controversies dealt with are entirely Christian. Indeed, the letters contain no Old Testament quotations. As we shall see, a mixture of ethical and theological problems is addressed. The author repeatedly insists upon obedience to Jesus' commandment of love, as if some Christians ignore it. In the background also are Christians—perhaps the same ones— who, it would seem, deny the real humanity ("flesh") of Jesus (1 John 4:2–3; 2 John 7). The letters do not address the problem of Christianity and the Jews or Christianity and the world. Rather, they address problems that have arisen in the life and thought of the Christian community, problems of the church. Nevertheless, it is entirely possible that a single author could have shifted focus or perspective between Gospel and letters in light of changed circumstances.

Perhaps more telling are some subtle, but real, differences in theological perspective. The Gospel appears to call attention to the present and future relevance of Jesus for the church's problems. The First Epistle stresses the importance of the past, "an old commandment which you had from the beginning" (2:7). While there is really no conflict here, only a different slant on things, the differences do not end there. The letters manifest divergences in such major areas of theology as the nature of Christ's saving work, eschatology (especially the return of Christ), and the doctrine of the Holy Spirit.

12

As much as Gospel and Epistle may agree that Jesus reveals and accomplishes salvation for humankind, 1 John seems closer to the primitive preaching (e.g., 1 Cor. 15:3) in its emphasis on the saving effect of Jesus' death, indeed, of his blood (1 John 1:7; cf. 2:2). Although the death of Jesus is important in the Fourth Gospel, the Evangelist is unique in his stress upon Jesus' death as exaltation, and the new perspective on Jesus' ministry that, with the coming of the Spirit, it affords. The Gospel does have John the Baptist greet Jesus as the "Lamb of God, who takes away the sin of the world" (1:29), presumably alluding to a sacrificial effect, but it does not develop the saving work of Jesus in these terms.

The Gospel of John is also noted for its so-called realized eschatology. The salvation Jesus promises is already fulfilled in his own time, or perhaps more accurately in that of the believer. When Martha speaks of the resurrection of her brother Lazarus in the last day, Jesus says, "I am the resurrection and the life" (11:25). Repeatedly, Jesus stresses that eternal life is a present, as well as a future, possibility. When the question of the time of Jesus' return is finally raised, he seems to set it on one side (21:23). Jesus has already by then spoken of his return in spiritual terms; it is not a public event (14:22). By contrast, 1 John seems to revive the primitive Christian belief in the imminent return of Jesus and the last judgment (2:8; 2:28; 3:2). Yet eschatology is still being realized; the true light is already shining (2:8). Moreover, the appearance of opponents is seen to signal the arrival of the apocalyptically conceived last days, as the references to the Antichrist indicate (1 John 2:18; 2 John 7). For its part, the Gospel speaks more than once of a resurrection at the last day (e.g., 6:40), as well as life for the believer beyond death (11:25–26; 14:1–7). Nevertheless, its distinctive emphasis is rather on the presence of eternal life. As in the case of the blood atonement of Jesus, the Epistle seems to lay stress on a more primitive or traditional theological position.

With the doctrine of the Spirit, the differences may be somewhat more subtle. The Gospel has a rich and distinctive doctrine of the Spirit as *paraklētos,* counselor (RSV) or helper, according to which the Spirit-Paraclete continues and expands upon the revelation Jesus has brought, as if the Spirit were Jesus himself under a different form. What is said about the Spirit in the Epistle is not so much in disagreement as it is less well defined or developed. Moreover, Jesus himself is now called *paraklētos* (1 John 2:1; RSV: "advocate"). Interestingly enough, when the Spirit-Paraclete is first mentioned in the Gospel (14:16) we find "another *paraklētos*" (RSV: "Counselor"; NRSV, however, translates "Advocate"), in some agreement with 1 John 2:1. One might think that the Gospel really presupposes the Epistle. In fact, in each case we have noticed the Gospel appears to represent the more advanced or developed perspective, and some interpreters (e.g., Grayston) have suggested that the Gospel was written later than the letters.

Most commentators, ancient and modern (Schnackenburg, Marshall, Brown, Smalley), nevertheless believe the Gospel is earlier, principally because the letters, especially 1 John, clearly presuppose it or something very much like it. If the letters then seem to be retreating to an earlier or more conservative position, such a move is not without precedent in the history of Christian doctrine. Also, while the language and style of the two are similar, the Gospel is quite a bit clearer in form and manner of expression. At more than a few points, the Epistle is difficult or ambiguous. If we did not know the Gospel, it would be very obscure indeed. Brown has observed that this relative obscurity also bespeaks different authors for the Gospel and the letters. This is as significant an argument as those based on background, perspective, theology, or differences of language and style, many of which can be accounted for because of the differences of genre (Gospel or letter) or setting. In interpreting the letters we shall proceed on the assumption of the priority of the Gospel. Probably the letters were also written by a different author, but this point is not crucial for our commentary.

Conceivably, the letters themselves were not all written by the same author. Third John is a letter to a specific church about matters that were obviously real and pressing, which tends to authenticate its genuineness as a letter, whoever its author was. And if it were not the work of an apostolic or similar figure, why should it have been preserved at all? By way of contrast, 2 John seems a pale imitation of 1 John, intended to warn the faithful away from heretics, and its genuineness is thus called into question. It may be inferred that it is not the work of the writer who wrote 1 and presumably 3 John, and not a genuine letter addressed to a specific situation. Theories of multiple authorship abound. Nevertheless, that all three letters were not written by the same author, "the Elder," cannot be proved. Possibly a different author wrote each. (Recently, Judith Lieu, in her very acute monograph *The Second and Third Epistles of John,* has emphasized the tensions between the Gospel and letters, which raise the question of multiple authorship.) Yet the similarities of

14

style, language, and conceptuality militate against efforts to assign them to different authors. The assumption of a single author for all three suffices for their interpretation, and we shall work on that basis.

Was the Author of the Johannine Letters an Apostle?

These three brief writings from the early church have been known as the Epistles or letters of *John.* In the Christian tradition from the late second century onward, this John is taken to be the disciple of Jesus, the son of Zebedee and brother of James, who also wrote the Fourth Gospel and the Book of Revelation. We have already observed the problematic status of the thesis of common authorship. Nevertheless, it is fair to say that these five books gained canonical status, were recognized as scripture, in the belief that they were apostolic writings.

This belief was warranted, at least in the sense that all five are authoritative, both implicitly, in tone, and also occasionally explicitly, by quite specific claims (John 21:24f; Rev. 22:7, 18–19; cf. 1 John 1:4f.). Yet in what further sense they can be considered "apostolic" is a good question.

In common Christian parlance "apostolic" has usually meant association with, or originating from, one of the twelve apostles of Jesus or the Apostle Paul. We owe the common equation of the apostles with the Twelve principally to Luke, and even he is not entirely consistent, for he can refer to Paul and Barnabas as apostles (Acts 14:14), although neither was a disciple of Jesus. Paul, of course, understood himself as an apostle, principally because he had seen the Risen Lord and had founded churches on the basis of his witness to him (1 Cor. 9:1). He once refers to "all the apostles" as if they were a large group (1 Cor. 15:7) and apparently speaks of Andronicus and Junias (RSV) or Junia (NRSV), persons otherwise unheard of, as apostles (Rom. 16:7). (Because Junia is a common feminine name and the masculine form Junias is unprecedented, the NRSV is likely correct; the Greek can be construed either way.)

Probably in the beginning, *apostle* was a somewhat broader category than it came to be in later Christian generations. Nevertheless, it always had the meaning of authoritative emissary; the word *apostolos* actually means "one sent," presumably on a mission with a certain authority. Thus the earlier, broader meaning is significantly related to the later, narrower sense. Certainly the Johannine letters, and all the Johannine writings,

15

are apostolic in the earlier and broader sense. They speak with an authority that is both implicit and explicit.

Yet unlike Paul's letters, none of the Johannine writings claims to be the work of an apostle in the narrower sense of the term, much less the work of John, the son of Zebedee and brother of James, who was apparently an important figure in the earliest church. In the list of the Twelve in Mark 3:17 James and John were said to be surnamed by Jesus "Boanerges" or "sons of thunder," but both Matthew and Luke drop this enigmatic epithet, which does not correspond exactly to the appropriate Hebrew or Aramaic. Whatever this mysterious term's derivation, it links James and John, presumably as possessors of some extraordinary power. Later John appears as the companion of Peter in the early chapters of Acts (3–4), and Paul makes clear that John was with Peter and Jesus' brother James in Jerusalem in the early years (Gal. 2:9). Paul says that the three were known as "pillars," without elaborating on the term, which has become proverbial ("pillar of the church") in popular Christian usage. John then disappears from the scene in the New Testament, although we learn of the martyr death in Jerusalem of his brother James (Acts 12:2).

For more than a century after the demise of the first Christian generation, we have no sure word or evidence from or about John. Then rather suddenly, toward the end of the second century, we begin hearing about him again. Irenaeus, the bishop of Lyons and one of the first theologians of the church, makes much use of the Fourth Gospel and confidently attributes it to John the disciple. Interestingly enough, he never refers to him as the son of Zebedee, but it has been assumed, probably correctly, that he so regarded him. Irenaeus seems to have been most interested in defending the apostolicity and authority of the Gospel of John as an orthodox writing against the Gnostics, who were attempting to make use of it for their own purposes.

From the end of the second century onward, the Fourth Gospel, joined later by the letters and Revelation, gained wide, and ultimately universal, recognition as the work of John the Apostle, the disciple of the Lord, the son of Zebedee, and brother of James. Thus tradition identifies John with the Beloved Disciple of the Gospel, although the Beloved Disciple is never said to be John within the Gospel itself. On the other hand, the author of Revelation says explicitly that his name is

John (1:4, 9); yet, significantly, he never refers to himself as an apostle. In fact, he speaks of the apostles as if they were revered figures of the past (18:20; 21:14), not as if he were one of them. All the letters are anonymous, except that the author refers to himself as "the Elder" in 2 and 3 John. There is no such designation in 1 John, although the author clearly regards himself as an authoritative figure. Nevertheless, he uses no titles at all, neither apostle nor elder. The name "John" occurs, of course, in the titles of all five Johannine books as they now stand in the New Testament, but these titles were added later, probably at the point at which they began to be assembled in collections, or at least lists, of authoritative books.

In fact, these books may even have functioned as authoritative, and in a broader sense apostolic, before they were recognized as the work of John specifically. A case in point is the First Epistle of John. Early in the second century (c. 125–135) Bishop Polycarp of Smyrna wrote a letter to the church at Philippi in which he quoted copiously from many if not most of the writings of our New Testament. This letter is extremely important for understanding the growth of the New Testament as a collection of authoritative books, i.e., scripture. When Polycarp wrote, there was no New Testament as such, although the writings that were to compose it were already in use in churches. Quite clearly Polycarp knew and cited 1 John, although he does not refer to it by name (7:1; cf. 1 John 4:2–3 and 2 John 7; also 7:2; cf. 1 John 1:1–4), but except for Paul, Polycarp refers to none of the New Testament authors by name. Apparently he knew the Synoptic Gospels, although it is less clear that he knew the Gospel of John. The echo of the Epistle is clearer than any affinity with the Gospel.

Polycarp thus attests the use of authoritative Christian writings presumably regarded as apostolic but, aside from Paul, not their attribution to specific apostles. Perhaps even Polycarp did not know the name of the author of 1 John. Today we can either be satisfied with tradition and call him John, or frankly admit that we do not know his name. I would prefer to do both, that is, while admitting ignorance nevertheless stick with tradition and, for convenience's sake also, call him "John."

The long-standing, traditional Christian belief that the author of the Gospel was, in fact, the Apostle John doubtless owes much to its attribution to the Beloved Disciple (21:20, 24). This, together with other references to a reliable witness (19:35; cf.

17

1:14), suggests someone very close to Jesus, but obviously not Peter, who is a kind of rival of the Beloved Disciple. James, the other son of Zebedee, was known to have died early (Acts 12:2). So, of the three disciples closest to Jesus in the Synoptic Gospels, John is the sole remaining candidate. Yet no incident in which this John figures according to the Synoptic narratives is found in the Gospel of John, and the widespread equation of John with the Beloved Disciple must await the latter years of the second century. It is possible, however, to identify the venerable disciple, who lived to a ripe old age (21:23), not with the Apostle, but with the Elder who names himself the author of 2 and 3 John and was probably the author of 1 John as well. (In a controversial statement attributed to Papias, Eusebius reflects a distinction between the Apostle and the Elder John; *Ecclesiastical History* (hereafter *EH*) 3.39.3–4.) Moreover, the author of 1 John seems to speak of a firsthand relationship to Jesus (1:1–4) and to recall with personal authority the word or message that was from the beginning. Whether or not his name was John, it is tempting to see in this Elder the Beloved Disciple of the Gospel. Tempting as it may be, however, such an identification rests on conjecture, circumstantial evidence, and later tradition. In addition, there are the problems already noted that suggest the evangelist and authors of the letters were different people. The authorship of the Johannine Gospel and letters remains an enigma shrouded in mystery.

The Audience and Purpose of the Letters

The identity of the author aside, the letters of John afford, as we have already observed, remarkably few handholds for defining and understanding the specific settings for which they were written and the problems to which they were addressed. Obviously, 3 John addresses problems of church discipline and leadership in which a certain Diotrephes, who opposes the Elder, played a leading role. Equally apparent is the fact that 2 John underscores and supports the teaching of 1 John about the reality of Jesus' flesh and in so doing rejects the teaching of opponents. Therefore, clearly one major purpose of the letters is to lay down the true doctrine and defend it against proponents of the false.

Such doctrine is not, however, opposed merely in the abstract. Rather, specific opponents are in view. In 2 John the

Elder warns against having anything to do with them. In both 2 John and 1 John they are equated with the Antichrist(s) who is to appear in the last days. Furthermore, 1 John speaks of a schism in the community (2:19) and holds that the opponents are "of the world, . . . and the world listens to them" (4:5). Evidently, the community of Johannine Christians not only is threatened with heresy but also has undergone division. The Pauline Pastorals reflect a similar situation. Already in 1 Corinthians (chaps. 1—4) there were divisions in the church, but channels of communication were still open. In the Pastorals, however, as in the Johannine Epistles, lines of division have hardened, and any efforts at persuasion have long since given way to denunciation and exclusion.

Quite obviously 1 John criticizes the behavior of certain Christians. Some behavior, especially a failure to show love, is undesirable, indeed intolerable, among believers. Often situations are described with such pointedness and heat that it is scarcely possible to imagine anything other than that specific people or parties are in view. Thus, "If anyone says, 'I love God,' and hates his brother, he is a liar; for he who does not love his brother whom he has seen, cannot love God whom he has not seen" (4:20); or again, "If we say we have no sin, we deceive ourselves, and the truth is not in us" (1:8). In some cases John says "anyone," in others "we," and it is difficult to know whether this difference is significant. That is, is John in the one case describing opponents, or separatists, and in the other admonishing those with whom he still feels aligned? At this distance it is hard to be sure. What seems plain, however, is the reality of kinds of behavior that cannot be approved. Were they characteristic of the heretics he denounces as antichrists? Probably in the judgment of the author they were.

In 1 John we hear the central and characteristic themes of Christian theology and ethics sounded. The importance of the incarnation, Jesus' humanity, is emphasized. The reality of sin and the necessity of its confession are underscored, and the forgiveness found in the death of Jesus is extolled. The love commandment of Jesus is remembered. Its relationship to the prior love of God is emphasized. "We love, because he first loved us" (4:19). Those who accept God's love enter eternal life. All these themes and others ring true today as they did then. For the Christian they have an enduring validity. Yet although they are not occasional or contingent ideas, dependent on a

19

peculiar set of circumstances, they were in all likelihood written down by our author to confront and overcome a specific situation, specific problems, and a group of adversaries.

Raymond E. Brown, in *The Community of the Beloved Disciple* and in his commentary, has argued persuasively that these adversaries were, or had at one time been, closely related to the author of the Johannine letters and the Christian communities he represents. They were not, as in the case of some of Paul's opponents (those encountered in Galatians or 2 Corinthians, for example) interlopers from outside. Instead, they shared many of the same theological convictions and traditions; perhaps they even shared the same Gospel of John. Insofar as we can infer from these letters, especially 1 John, the beliefs and activities of these adversaries, they seem to have been distortions—or what we and the author of 1 John would regard as distortions—of theological positions or attitudes of the Fourth Gospel. Thus, for example, the heavy emphasis on the visibility, and even tangibility, of Jesus in the prologue of 1 John makes clear where the emphasis of the prologue of the Gospel (John 1:1–18) should be placed. The point is not so much the appearance of the revealer among us, or the manifestation of his glory (*doxa*, a term that occurs frequently in the Gospel, but not at all in the letters of John), as the reality of the incarnation. The word really became flesh and dwelt among us. One who understood this would confess that Jesus Christ had come in the flesh (1 John 4:2; cf. 2 John 7) and would not think of denying so fundamental a truth.

In the face of those who claim that they cannot sin, or are already free from sin and death (cf. John 3:18, 21; 5:24; 8:31–35), the author of 1 John finds it necessary to insist on the importance of the confession of sin and of continuing forgiveness (1:8–9; 2:1–2). Moreover, like Paul he looks forward to the day when Jesus will return (1 John 2:28; 3:2–3). Yet that anticipation contains within it a subtle but unmistakable sense of tension, shared with many other early Christians: "And now, little children, abide in him, so that when he appears we may have confidence and not shrink from him in shame at his coming" (2:28; cf. 1 Cor. 3:10–15; 2 Cor. 5:10). One cannot rest on laurels already won, even by Christ himself. The believer must live in obedience to Christ: in particular he or she must accept and obey the commandment to love. The author of 1 John never tires of insisting on this. As we read through the letter, it will

20

be worthwhile for us to note how often its themes can be understood as an underscoring of, or an insisting upon, truths or commands already known from the Gospel; that is, known to us, probably also known to the author, and quite possibly known to the adversaries the author has in view.

As to the time and place in which the letters of John were written, certainty is unattainable. Nevertheless, a reasonable estimate can be made. If the letters were composed after the Gospel, they would scarcely be earlier than the last decade of the first century. (According to tradition, John was the last of the canonical Gospels written.) The harking back to the beginning of the Christian tradition that is characteristic of 1 John also suggests the passage of a number of years, as does the rise of what was later called heresy (1 John 4:1–6; 2 John 7). There is no way to determine the place of origin or destination. The tradition that links the Gospel, and by implication the letters, with Ephesus in Asia Minor is at least plausible. The more remotely related Revelation to John was written on the nearby island of Patmos (Rev. 1:9). Determination of place is less germane to the content and meaning of the letters than that of time. Some remoteness from the time of Jesus and the first Christian preaching seems to be presupposed, and such a setting makes the content of the letters more intelligible.

The Composition and Structure of the Letters

In the case of 2 John or 3 John, questions of composition and structure are not complex. Each is easily comprehended as a letter containing a relatively simple message, perhaps with more than one aspect, written at a single sitting without the use of written sources. Probably 2 John presupposes 1 John, as 1 John presupposes the Gospel. Although 3 John is illumined by the other letters, as well as by the Gospel, it is not so closely related to them. How the relatively few parts of each letter relate to one another is not hard to see, even though, in the case of 3 John particularly, we need to exercise imagination in order to understand the relationships of the issues and persons mentioned.

1 John is, however, an entirely different matter. The process of composition that lay behind, and produced, the letter is not obvious and consequently is a matter of dispute among scholars. This is not altogether surprising, inasmuch as that process is

now hidden from us and must be deduced from the present text or what we can infer about it. The text, of course, is immediately accessible to us. Nevertheless, its structure, or structuring principle, is by no means obvious. Even a cursory examination of commentaries reveals considerable disagreement on the basic divisions of the text and where individual pericopes (or paragraphs) are to be demarcated. (Of course, the most ancient manuscripts have no paragraph divisions, much less the chapter or verses that were a medieval invention.) In his commentary Brown has summarized in a chart representative divisions of the Epistle by more than three dozen modern commentators (p. 764), and they represent an astonishing variety.

The question of structure requires further attention, but it is worth observing that the lack of a clear or obvious structure or structuring principle has led a number of scholars to raise questions about the process of composition. Perhaps the structure is unclear because the author or authors used earlier sources or subjected an original text to editing and emendation. Thus any unclarity or confusion in the present text is the result of overlap of sources and redaction.

Among such proposals, Rudolf Bultmann's are probably the best known. They are set forth in several articles and are most accessible in the English translation of his commentary in the Hermeneia series. Readers of Bultmann's *The Gospel of John: A Commentary* will not be surprised at his procedure and proposals in the exegesis of 1 John. For the Epistle as for the Gospel, Bultmann posits a gnostic or gnosticlike sayings source in a rhythmic or strophic style, which has been edited by the author as he incorporated it into his own work. Such a basic editorial process has then been further complicated by a secondary editing or redaction intended to express the interests and emphases of an emerging ecclesiastical orthodoxy. Thus, for example, clear references to the future return of Jesus, or accompanying apocalyptic events, are assigned to this latest redactional stage (1 John 2:28; possibly 3:2; cf. John 5:28–29), along with any mention of sacraments (1 John 5:7–8; cf. John 6:51c–58). Moreover, in his commentary on the Epistles, Bultmann proposes that 2:28—5:12 "is obviously not a coherent organic composition, but rather a compendium of various fragments collected as a supplement to 1:5—2:27" (pp. 43–44). Bultmann attempts no distinction of source or authorship in this connection but rather thinks that the original author's sketches or meditations (and, he adds parenthetically and, I think, facetiously, reports from sessions of his seminar) may have been collected and added by his disciples, that is, by the Johannine school.

Because Bultmann attempts to attain a kind of precision that is in the nature of the case impossible, his arguments have failed to persuade other interpreters in the case of 1 John as in that of the Gospel. Nevertheless, his suggestions are not outlandish and in principle are perhaps correct. That is, the present state of the text may well result from a rather complex process of composition involving earlier traditions and perhaps drafts. Other, subsequent, commentators, such as Houlden (pp. 24–25), have suggested that such deposits of teaching and preaching were brought together in 1 John as in the Gospel, albeit in a process we can no longer trace in any detail or with any certainty. Interestingly enough, neither Bultmann nor Houlden attempts to delineate a hierarchical structure or outline of 1 John beyond simple divisions of the text. (That is, they do not distinguish major divisions of the text from subsections under those divisions, etc.)

In this commentary I have followed the same procedure, if for somewhat different reasons. I began by simply working on the individual pericopes or paragraphs of the RSV, thinking that in the process a structure and hierarchy would become apparent and that such a structure or outline could then be superimposed on what had been done. That has not, however, proved to be the case, and it seemed unwise to force the issue. There is, however, one proposal for structuring the Epistle that seems to me to be sound and, moreover, based upon an important insight about the nature of 1 John and its purpose. It does not require that we believe the author very carefully or self-consciously developed a finely articulated structure, and it commends itself for that reason.

On good grounds, Brown has proposed that 1 John is to be interpreted over against, even as it interprets, the Gospel of John. If this be true, it may have implications for the structure of the Epistle. "If the epistolary author is drawing upon the theology and wording of the Johannine tradition embodied in the Gospel of John and assumes the mantle of the evangelist as an interpreter of that tradition (the 'we' of the Johannine school), *a priori* it is not inconceivable that he used the Gospel of John as a model in structuring his comments in 1 John" (Brown, p. 124). How or where may the role of the Gospel in

23

the structuring of 1 John be seen? Obviously, there is a distinct and apparently intentional paralleling of 1 John 1:1–4 with John 1:1–18. In addition, there are parallel conclusions in John 21 and 1 John 5:13(14)–21. Brown speaks of the epilogue of the Gospel but does not want to use that term of the Epistle, since he believes it is not from a later hand. However that may be, the parallelism is real enough. Most commentators agree on the demarcation of these beginning and ending sections.

Within the Epistle, however, where may the lines be drawn? Now the judgments of commentators vary considerably. Almost all agree that 4:1–6 (the discerning of spirits) is a discrete section, but there are not many other instances in which there is such wide agreement. Brown proposes a major division within the body of the Epistle after 3:10, for in 3:11 the author again writes, as he did in 1:5, and only there, "This is the message which you have heard from the beginning" (or, as in 1:5, "we have heard from him and proclaim to you"). Brown translates *angelia* as "gospel" rather than "message," which stretches the Greek a bit, since "gospel" usually renders *euangelion,* but his point is valid. Beginning in 1:5 and again in 3:11 John sets forth and reiterates the heart of the gospel as he understands it. In 1:5—3:10 there is a kind of parallel to John chapters 2—12, where confrontation with the opposition (in the Gospel "the Jews," in 1 John the secessionists) is primarily in view, while in 3:11—5:12 attention centers on loving relationships within the community of disciples, as is the case in the latter half of the Gospel.

Following this arrangement makes sense of the content of the two major parts of the Epistle. The second is reminiscent of the first, but there is also a subtle shift in nuance or emphasis. The second does not simply repeat the first. Thus one is not driven, as Bultmann was in his commentary, to the expedient of regarding the last three chapters as addenda representing no progression of thought beyond the first two. Nevertheless, such progression as one finds is not driven by any tight logic. Rather, the movement of thought is related to the situation of opposition the author faces, as well as the substance of the Gospel, which is the ground of his inspiration and authority. Later on in this introduction (pp. 26–30) other aspects of the relationship of 1 John to the Gospel will be discussed.

The Use of the Letters of John in the Church

Along with the other Johannine letters, 1 John is tradition-ally grouped among the Catholic (or general) Epistles of the New Testament (the others being James, 1 and 2 Peter, and Jude). The Catholic Epistles are so called because they are not addressed to particular churches, like the Pauline letters, but to wider circles of churches or—as it sometimes appears—to all Christians everywhere. The designation goes back to the fourth century, and probably even earlier, for the church his-torian Eusebius, writing in the early part of that century, says that these letters were already being called *katholikai* (*EH* 2.23.25).

We have seen that at least 1 John was known to Polycarp and regarded as authoritative during the first half of the second century. Furthermore, Eusebius says that Papias, an early Christian writer of the same period, was familiar with the First Epistle (*EH* 3.39.17). It is possible that other Christian writings from mid-second century—for example, *The Epistle of Barna-bas* (5:9–11), the *First Apology* of Justin Martyr (32.7), and the *Epistle to Diognetus* (10:2–3; 11:4)—reflect some knowledge of 1 John (see Brown, pp. 6–9.) Toward the end of the second century, Irenaeus, who knew the Fourth Gospel as the work of John the disciple, cites 1 and 2 John and attributes them to the same author (*Against Heresies* 3.16.5, 8; cf. 1.16.3; Eusebius, *EH* 5.8.7, attests Irenaeus's acceptance of 1 John). Other Christian writers such as Clement and Tertullian soon followed, at least in the use of 1 and 2 John. Not until mid-third century, however, is 3 John attested in our extant sources. Apparently, Origen knew 3 John as well as 2 John but also recognized that not all Christians, or church authorities, regarded them as genuine (Eusebius, *EH* 6.25.10). Thus even in the early fourth century Eusebius listed 1 John among the generally accepted New Tes-tament books but had to acknowledge that 2 and 3 John were still disputed by some (*EH* 3.24.17–18; cf. 3.25.2–3). Brown (p. 12) notes that even such worthies as John Chrysostom and Theodore of Mopsuestia, who lived into the fifth century, did not cite 2 or 3 John as scripture. These letters are, of course, included in the canonical list of the Festal Letter of Athanasius (A.D. 367), which is the first such list to accord exactly with the New Testament as we know it today.

The fact that 1 John, and to a lesser degree 2 John, achieved earlier recognition than 3 John does not say very much about the question of authorship or about their subsequent authority and canonical status. One might infer some doubt in antiquity about whether 2, and especially 3 John, were the work of the same apostolic author as 1 John and the Gospel. Apparently there was doubt in some quarters, but probably not on what we would consider historical-critical grounds. Both 2 and 3 John are quite brief, the shortest books in the New Testament, or in the Bible for that matter. This alone may have been a negative factor, counting against their recognition as canonical books. Moreover, the meaning and significance of the letters may no longer have been entirely clear. About a third of 2 John consists of pro forma epistolary salutation and conclusion. The brief body of the letter largely repeats emphases of 1 John (vv. 4–7) and warns the readers to abjure false doctrine and those who disseminate it (vv. 8–11), a point made also at greater length in 1 John, although the latter does not have the prohibition against receiving or greeting heretics.

On the other hand, 3 John is not so repetitive of 1 John (or 2 John) but is concerned rather with concrete and particular matters as they affect a specific church. (Only in 3 John, among the Gospel and letters, is the word *ekklēsia,* "church," used.) Specific persons are also named: Gaius, to whom the letter is addressed (v. 1); Diotrephes, with whom the Elder has a dispute (vv. 9–10); Demetrius, who is commended (v. 12; cf. Paul's reference to letters of recommendation in 2 Cor. 3:1–3). In later years, such individual persons and specific, apparently nondoctrinal matters would no longer have much importance. Quite possibly, questions about 3 John's usefulness might have brought its genuineness, or at least its authority, into question.

Interpreting the Johannine Letters in Light of the Gospel of John and the New Testament Generally

The question about whether, as tradition holds, the Gospel and letters were written by the same author has already been noted and discussed. Yet however the historical relationship may be assessed, there are obvious and important similarities or affinities between the Johannine letters and the Fourth Gospel, some of which we have already noted in discussing the composition and structure of 1 John.

26

The similarities begin, of course, with the prologue of 1 John (1:1–4), which reads very much like the prologue of the Gospel. The initial reference to the beginning, Jesus as the word (or word of life), the emphasis on testimony or witness, eternal life, the Father and the Son—all are reminiscent of, and probably derived from, the prologue of the Gospel. Moreover, the dualism of the Gospel—especially such polarities as light and darkness, love and hate, truth and falsehood—is characteristic also of the letters, especially 1 John. Also the *new commandment* of Jesus to love one another (John 13:34) turns up in 1 John as the old, but also the new, commandment (1 John 2:7–8), and it is again quite clearly the love commandment of Jesus "which you had from the beginning" (cf. 3:11). Similarly, 1 John, like the Gospel, emphasizes the importance of abiding in Jesus, the Son, as well as in the Father (2:24, 27; 3:6, etc.).

All in all, there is a remarkable similarity of style and overlap of vocabulary between the letters and the Gospel, a similarity so remarkable it scarcely needs further documentation here (see Brown, pp. 20–21, 757–759; cf. 755–756). To put matters graphically, the style and vocabulary of Jesus' speech as portrayed in John's Gospel are closer to the Johannine letters than to the Jesus of the Synoptic Gospels. It is unlikely, of course, that Jesus spoke in the style and vocabulary of the Gospel and letters of John, as distinguished from the Synoptics. More likely, these writings reflect the speech of a circle of early Christians inspired by Jesus, who nevertheless have found their own distinctive way of expressing themselves.

Despite the obvious differences between the language and thought-forms of the synoptic Jesus and those of the Gospel and letters of John, both of the latter reflect the conviction that this Jesus to whom they appeal is very important, indeed fundamental, for faith. Apart from Jesus, there is no longer any true faith in God. Jesus is for them no pious fiction or figment of the imagination but the historically real and physically visible and palpable manifestation of God (John 1:14; 1 John 1:1–4). Who then is this Jesus? How is he conceived or understood?

Christians likely read the letters, as well as the Gospel of John, in light of a figure of Jesus etched into our consciousness from many sources, including the Synoptic Gospels and Paul, not to mention a tradition nearly two thousand years old. Jesus is referred or alluded to frequently in 1 John, often in an enigmatic way: "That which was from the beginning" (1:1); "you

27

have been anointed by the Holy One" (2:20); "when he appears we shall be like him" (3:2); "this is the message which you have heard from the beginning" (3:11). It should not be surprising that the many appeals to Jesus found in 1 John are read by Christians in light of the New Testament generally, as well as of later tradition. Indeed, the shape of the canon makes such a reading seem natural and proper. Yet when the author of 1 John appealed to Jesus, what portrait of Jesus did he have in view? Probably the one we find in the Fourth Gospel. There is no convincing evidence that the author of the Johannine letters was fundamentally influenced by either the Synoptic Gospels or Paul. On the other hand, as we have noted, there is every reason to think that he knew either the Gospel of John or the traditions we find in it. At least he knew the Johannine Jesus, if not the Johannine Gospel. Probably he knew both.

When the reader familiar with the New Testament encounters the prologue of 1 John or that letter's play upon the dialectic of old and new commandments, he will naturally think of the prologue of the Fourth Gospel or Jesus' new commandment (13:34; 15:12). But unless the question is raised, the reader will not likely try to imagine what perception or understanding of those passages in 1 John there would be, or could be, apart from the Fourth Gospel. In fact, the prologue of the letter would likely seem unintelligible, and even ungrammatical, if we did not read it with knowledge of the Gospel's prologue. Something of the sort might also be said about the commandment (of love) that is said to be both old and new. The Gospel provides a meaningful context for otherwise enigmatic statements of 1 John. Reading 1 John 2:7–8, we immediately get the point that the commandment of love is old in the sense that it goes back to the beginning (Jesus), but new in that it marks a new age and new conditions in which light displaces darkness. Readers of 1 John alone might get that meaning, but only dimly. They would miss its subtlety and richness if they did not know the Gospel.

Thus 1 John presupposes familiarity with the Christian message and tradition as it is known from the Gospel of John or something substantially like it. This is confirmed not only by the instances cited above but by the nature and emphasis of their respective Christologies. In the Gospel of John Jesus frequently refers to himself as the Son of God, his Father, and even speaks openly of his descent from heaven (cf. 6:38, 40):

28

> For I have come down from heaven, not to do my own will, but the will of him who sent me; . . . . For this is the will of my Father, that every one who sees the Son and believes in him should have eternal life; and I will raise him up at the last day (6:38, 40).

> For God so loved the world that he gave his only Son, that whoever believes in him should not perish but have eternal life (3:16).

These ideas are not without precedent in the rest of the New Testament. After all, Jesus not infrequently speaks of God as Father in the Synoptic Gospels, and Paul writes, "when the time had fully come, God sent forth his Son" (Gal. 4:4; cf. Phil. 2:5–11). But their terminology, frequency, and clear christological focus and intensity are paralleled nowhere so much as in the Johannine letters:

> In this the love of God was made manifest among us, that God sent his only Son into the world, so that we might live through him (4:9).

> And we have seen and testify that the Father has sent his Son as the Savior of the world (4:14).

While 1 John does not expressly refer to Jesus' descent from heaven, its Christology seems to presuppose such an advent and is in that and other ways parallel to, or congruent with, the Christology of the Gospel.

Yet, interestingly enough, after one has read through and pondered the New Testament and, near the end, encounters the Johannine letters, they seem to resonate in a truly remarkable harmony not only with the Gospel of John, but with the New Testament generally. The statements of John Wesley in the eighteenth century that "my beloved children" includes "the whole body of Christians" and of W. G. Kümmel in the twentieth that "the entirety of Christianity is being addressed" seem appropriate. They may not, in fact, be true historically, that is, true with respect to the intention of the author or the scope of the audience he had in view at the time of writing. Nevertheless, Wesley and Kümmel correctly sense the potential scope of the text and of the audience addressed by it. Obviously, John no more anticipates twentieth-century readers than does Paul. Yet contemporary readers, now as then, acknowledge his words as true, in the faith that the christological, soteriological, and ethical claims he makes are valid and pressing claims upon us. Put more simply, "Jesus Christ is the same yesterday and today and for ever" (Heb. 13:8), in the demands he places upon us as well as the salvation he effects. These claims are seldom acknowledged by an individual in isolation. He or she comes to such acknowledgment in and through a community, which induces faith by its witness. According to John, that witness consists of mutual relationships and deeds as well as words (13:35, 1 John 3:17; 4:20). Moreover, faith is perceived as a gift, not a "work" in the sense of achievement. Thus the importance of the Spirit is emphasized both by the Gospel (e.g., 14:15–17; 16:13) and 1 John (3:24; 4:13).

Because of the multidimensional relationships of the letters, our policy in exposition will be first to relate specific statements to other statements or dimensions of these letters, then to show their background in the Gospel of John, and finally to call attention to the ways in which they evoke aspects of the New Testament message generally.

A Word About This Commentary

Following the policy of the Interpretation series, this commentary will be based on the Revised Standard Version. Obviously, this translation, like any other, embodies decisions about syntax and meaning. To base the commentary on the RSV means insofar as possible accepting those decisions, but other possible translations that may contribute to resolving difficulties are discussed.

After the text of the commentary was written, the New Revised Standard Version appeared. Because millions of copies of the RSV will remain in use, and it will continue to be printed and distributed, we have decided not to attempt to change the basis of this commentary. Nevertheless, the NRSV of the Johannine letters has been compared with the RSV, as well as with the Greek text (Nestle-Aland, *Novum Testamentum Graece*, 26th ed.). Where the NRSV offers a clearly superior translation, that has been noted. Of course, the NRSV offers a clearly superior translation, that has been noted. Of course, the NRSV translators made a special effort to use gender-inclusive language. This is a delicate issue, for in ancient Greek, as in modern English, the masculine gender generally stood for both men and women, and this was universally known and accepted. Thus *adelphoi*

30

(brothers) was applied to brothers and sisters, "he who confesses" meant "he or she who confesses," and the like. Probably
such usage reflected the dominance of the male sex, although
it also made for a certain economy of expression that is sometimes lost in the NRSV. Occasionally, the NRSV's changes made
in the interest of inclusive language have been noted.

We also follow RSV paragraphing (with few exceptions
adopted also in the NRSV), which is more appropriate to the
meaning or sense of the letters than, for example, the pericopes
of the Common Lectionary, which is doubtless familiar to many
users of this commentary. The latter are, of course, intended to
serve a liturgical rather than an exegetical purpose, and the
divisions of the text of 1 John were apparently determined in
part with a view to their coordination with other appointed
lessons. In the Common Lectionary, only 1 John appears. The
brief 2 and 3 John are omitted, as is Jude. The content of 2 and
3 John is not only brief, but, like Jude, reflects controversy,
whether theological (2 John) or political and jurisdictional (3
John). Certainly controversy is an essential and integral element of the letters; they cannot be adequately understood apart
from it. One might judge them unedifying for homiletical or
liturgical use for that reason. Yet precisely out of such controversy 2 and 3 John raise issues worthy of theological and ethical
reflection because they are pertinent to Christian life and
thought.

The Common Lectionary readings from 1 John cover the
second through the seventh Sundays of Easter in the B cycle.
In addition, John 3:1–3 (also represented in Easter 3B) is the
Epistle lesson for All Saints' Day in the A cycle. The lessons
included are 1:1—2:2; 3:1–7; 3:18–24; 4:7–12; 5:1–6; 5:9–13.
Again, the more noteworthy controversy passages—for example, the Antichrist passage beginning in 2:18 and the warning
to test the spirits (4:1–6)—do not appear. One is surprised, however, not to find 4:13–21, which is an apt summary of the theology and ethics of 1 John, indeed of the Johannine literature
generally. Yet everything could not be included, and 1 John is
as well represented in the Common Lectionary as writings of
comparable length, for example, Galatians, 2 Thessalonians,
and James.

Without ignoring the Lectionary, this commentary will
focus principally on the text of the letters themselves. Insofar
as a context of interpretation is needed, we have already indi-

31

cated that we shall find it first of all in the other Johannine writings, the Epistles and the Gospel, but also in the rest of the New Testament. That the letters were written with knowledge of the Gospel, or of its traditions and theological perspective, is a safe assumption. While one may not assume that the letters agree with the Gospel of John in every respect, the Gospel delimits the theological field upon which they play. Furthermore, at least 2 John seems to presuppose 1 John, although the relationship of 3 John to the other letters is less clear.

Bibliographical Reflection

Because the Johannine letters invite comment, commentaries on them are not in short supply. The most up-to-date technical commentaries in English are those of Raymond E. Brown and Stephen S. Smalley, both of which are based on the Greek text. (In line with the policy of the Anchor Bible, Brown offers his own translation of the Greek, which is discussed fully in the notes.) Somewhat less technical, but nonetheless reputable, are the recent commentaries of Kenneth Grayston, J. L. Houlden, I. Howard Marshall, and Pheme Perkins. From earlier generations there are the more technical commentaries of Rudolf Bultmann (translated for the Hermeneia series) and A. E. Brooke (International Critical Commentary) as well as shorter commentaries by the well-known British and American scholars C. H. Dodd and Amos Wilder, respectively. In German there is also the commentary of Rudolf Schnackenburg, kept current through many editions, as well as the quite recent work of Georg Strecker, which has replaced Bultmann in the Meyer series.

Each of these commentaries is reliable and worth consulting, although they naturally represent different points of view. The distinctive contribution of this commentary lies not in the area of historical-critical method, which is, of course, taken quite seriously, but in its purpose and focus. The Interpretation series as a whole is consciously and explicitly intended to be useful to teachers and preachers in the Christian church. Thus it happily accords with the intention and purpose of the Johannine letters themselves, which are clearly addressed to problems and issues having to do with the church's preaching and teaching. This agreement in purpose, and even genre, between commentary and text should in some important ways make for a felicitous interpretation, even from an historical-critical perspective.

This is an outstanding Epistle. It can buoy up afflicted hearts. Furthermore, it has John's style and manner of expression, so beautifully and gently does it picture Christ to us.

(Martin Luther, *Lectures on the First Epistle of St. John*)

THE BOOK OF
First John

1 John 1:1–4
Prologue: What Has Been Heard, Seen, and Touched

Every reader familiar with the Gospel of John recognizes the relation of the letter's prologue to that of the Gospel. The important theological terms and concepts are the same or similar; there is a significant overlap of theological vocabularies. Nevertheless, there are also significant differences, and we shall have to attend to both. Strangely, these differences from the Gospel do not immediately distinguish 1 John as a letter, for there is no conventional greeting.

Although we speak of the Johannine letters, only 2 and 3 John have epistolary salutations and endings. On the other hand, 1 John not only begins like the Gospel but ends abruptly (5:21). Still, the author immediately indicates he is writing to someone (1:4; cf. 2:12). This is a written communication from a Christian leader—he never identifies himself by name or title—to other Christians, presumably a community or church. (In 2 and 3 John the author in the salutation immediately names himself "the Elder," and in 3 John he also makes it quite explicit that he is addressing a church.)

It may well be that 1 John lacks an epistolary opening precisely in order to evoke the Gospel. Instead of a greeting we find a prologue. By emulating the form of the Gospel's prologue, the writer immediately calls the reader's attention to the importance of the relationship of what he is writing to the Gospel. Thus the Epistle immediately evokes and recalls the Gospel, and the priority of the Gospel becomes clear.

Why not the other way around? That is, why should we not regard the Gospel's prologue as a development of the more or less inchoate expression of 1 John? In ways we shall observe, the prologue of 1 John becomes intelligible on the basis of the Gospel, but without the Gospel 1 John 1:1–4 would be a most enigmatic text. It is over-full and digressive; the syntax is not immediately clear. (Verse 2 might well have been set within parentheses, although the RSV chose dashes.) In light of the Gospel we immediately sense what John 1:1–4 is about, and, indeed, the passage becomes intelligible, not only in itself, but as a kind of commentary upon John 1:1–14.

The very opening phrase "that which was from the beginning" seems to echo John 1:1 "in the beginning," but there is an important difference. John 1:1 begins a narrative, strange and mysterious though it may be, about the Word (Greek: *logos*), its being and function with God and its journey into human life and history. It presupposes nothing except the reader's attention and familiarity with the terms. Without explicitly saying so, 1 John 1:1 seems to assume the narrative of the Gospel and comment upon it. Only at the end of verse 1 does the reader learn that the pronouns ("that which," "which"; NRSV adopts the more idiomatic English "what") refer to "the word of life." Here two fundamental concepts, *word* and *life*, familiar from the prologue of the Gospel, are brought together. As John 1:4 makes clear that the Word brought and brings life, so 1 John appropriately brings the two terms together. Yet in verse 2 the subject of the sentence is no longer the word but life. The Christian reader, at least the reader familiar with the Gospel of John, will immediately recognize that "life" has become a way of referring to Jesus.

By writing "word of life," 1 John evokes another possible reading or understanding. In early Christian vocabulary, "the word" (or word of God) is also the gospel message, the good news about Jesus Christ and the salvation brought through him (Acts 4:4; Phil. 1:14; 1 Thess. 1:6). So the "word of life" is at once a reference to Jesus the Word who is the origin of life and an allusion to the preaching about him. That preaching or message is alluded to in the following verse (v. 2: "testify to it") and explicitly mentioned in verse 5. (It is worth noticing that RSV and NRSV capitalize "Word" in John 1:1 but not in 1 John 1:1, perhaps reflecting the fact that it is clearly a title of Jesus in the Gospel but not so clearly so in the Epistle.)

36

"The beginning" in the Gospel (1:1) manifestly is the cosmic beginning, primordial time, so to speak. Here that sense may be alluded to, but emphasis immediately shifts to Christian beginnings. Thus 1 John speaks of what has been heard, seen, looked upon, and touched. The reader remembers the climactic affirmation of John 1:14: "The Word became flesh and dwelt among us." Probably that is exactly what the author intended. In several ways 1 John's prologue and the statements following it refer to the incarnation, as Christian theology will call it, and invite the reader to reflect upon its nature and importance.

The parenthetical verse 2, set off by dashes in RSV, describes "the life," which is the content of the word (v. 1), and emphasizes its manifestation, its having been seen, and the testimony that is borne to it. The NRSV speaks of life's being "revealed," as the Greek verb *phaneroun* is consistently so translated. The life is further defined as the eternal life that was with God (cf. John 1:4). Eternal life as something other than physical, biological life is a recurring theme of the Fourth Gospel particularly and is not foreign to the rest of the New Testament (see Mark 10:17), although the term "eternal life" is less frequent elsewhere. Jesus is the bringer of eschatological life, the life that is final but without end, the life of God's new age.

The emphasis on seeing, hearing, and proclamation continues (v. 3) as a new concept, *fellowship* (Greek: *koinōnia*), is introduced. Only now do we find a finite verb ("we proclaim") in the prologue, a deficiency that the NRSV remedies by beginning "We declare . . ." (v. 1). (Yet in so doing it obscures the initial parallelism with the prologue of the Gospel.) Fellowship may be understood as communion, participation, or partnership. It is set out here as the goal of the proclamation of the gospel. This fellowship is, so to speak, vertical as well as horizontal. That is, it is fellowship with God and Christ and fellowship among people. God in the Johannine literature is very frequently referred to as Father. This is a heritage of Jewish and of Old Testament tradition, but it is also a reflection of Jesus' own teaching in the Synoptic Gospels as well as John. In the Johannine writings the fatherhood of God is constantly set over against the sonship of Jesus and is a way of expressing their most intimate relationship. This relationship is entered into and shared by believers. It can be called *koinōnia*, fellowship, but it can also be spoken of in other ways, particularly in terms of abiding in God or Jesus (cf. 2:6, 10; John 14:10–11, 23; 15:7–10). There is a mutual indwelling among Father (God), Son (Christ), and believers that constitutes their fellowship. This fellowship is, to use common Christian parlance, the church—although the

37

term occurs only in the Third Epistle. Interestingly enough, the term "fellowship" is not found in the Gospel, although the idea of mutual abiding or indwelling occurs rather frequently. Thus in the Gospel Jesus' final prayer stresses the importance of the oneness or unity of believers in God and Christ (17:21, 23; cf. 10:16). Still, the rich concept of *koinōnia* (fellowship) belongs to 1 John and distinguishes it in the New Testament. (Otherwise, *koinōnia* appears a dozen or more times in Paul's letters.) The NRSV emphasizes the importance of this fellowship: *"Truly our fellowship is with the Father and with his Son Jesus Christ."* Although "truly" translates no Greek word, the emphasis is valid.

The brief prologue of the letter ends on the role of joy (v. 4). John writes in order that "our" (or "your," depending on the manuscript reading followed) joy may be complete or fulfilled, again a typically Johannine idea. Interestingly enough, in the parable of the true vine in the Gospel an emphasis on abiding in Jesus and his love (15:7–10) is also followed immediately by the promise of joy (v. 11). In all probability the existence of a similar pattern in the Gospel and 1 John 1:3–4 is not coincidental: Abiding in Jesus or his (and God's) love leads to the ultimate, eschatological joy that is eternal life, the proper goal and fruition of human existence.

As clearly as 1 John 1:1–4 evokes the themes of the prologue of the Gospel, it is both more and less than a commentary on it. Aspects of the Gospel's prologue do not appear here at all. The role of the Word or Logos in creation (John 1:1–5, 10) is at most alluded to in 1 John 1:1. There is no mention of John the Baptist (John 1:6–8, 15). The theme of light (John 1:4–5, 9) does not figure in 1 John 1:1–4, although it appears later (1 John 2:8–11). Neither does the rejection of Jesus by his people (John 1:11). The Gospel prologue's related themes of becoming children of God (v. 12), and being born of God (v. 13), while not mentioned in 1 John 1:1–4, are, however, encountered later (3:9–10). The fact that no one has seen God (John 1:18) is not mentioned in 1 John's prologue, but there is nevertheless a reflection of this theme in 4:12, 20.

In sum, 1 John 1:1–4 is reminiscent of John 1:1–18 but falls short of being a commentary on all of it. The Epistle's prologue seems to presuppose the Gospel's but manifests a particular interest only in certain aspects of it. What concerns 1 John particularly is the Gospel's claim that the Word became flesh and dwelt among us (1:14). In fact, most of 1 John 1:1–4 can be understood as an elaboration of this theme. It is probably significant that although in 1:14 the Gospel writer claims to speak on behalf of those who have beheld the incarnate Word's glory *(doxa),* there is no mention of this glory in 1 John's prologue—or in the whole letter for that matter. (In fact, one scarcely glimpses in 1 John the biblical motifs, drawn from Genesis, the Exodus tradition, Isaiah, and elsewhere, that underlie the Gospel.) John does not now wish to emphasize the beholding of Christ's glory so much as the simple realities of hearing, seeing, and touching, followed by testifying or proclaiming. Primarily, John has in view the visibility and palpability of the Word become flesh.

Apparently, 1 John lays down the lines along which John 1:14 should be interpreted. The Word's becoming flesh means that Jesus Christ was a real human being, real flesh. The Gospel (1:14) seems to mean this but moves very quickly from the affirmation that the Word became flesh to the claim to have seen his glory. The Epistle, on the other hand, dwells upon the reality of Jesus' flesh. Jesus was not only audible and visible but tangible. Later on the confession that Jesus has come in the flesh is affirmed, while those who refuse to confess this are condemned as antichrists (4:2–3; 2 John 7). Has the opposition that John faced led him to define the nature and meaning of Christ's appearing, that is, of the incarnation, more precisely? It would seem so. No longer does it suffice to confess that the Word became flesh. Now the genuineness of that fleshliness must be underscored. If no mention is made of the revelation of the glory, that can be assumed. Probably the opponents agree that the revelation of God in Jesus was glorious.

Quite possibly an emphasis on Christ's glory has led to a diminution of his humanity. If so, we are witness to (or overhearing) an intra-Johannine debate, in the sense that this is an argument about how the central or climactic affirmation of the Gospel's prologue is to be understood. Is the emphasis to fall on Christ's glory in such a way that his humanity is in effect set aside, or is the reality of his fleshly existence the point that must be adhered to at all costs? Obviously 1 John affirms the latter, in all probability against those who would take the interpretation of the Gospel of John in a diametrically opposed direction.

39

The implications of this passage for Christian teaching are clear enough. We are dealing with a crucial aspect of what has since been called the doctrine of the incarnation. What is at stake here? In 1 John we find a definitive answer to the question of the nature of Jesus and his coming, set out over against a teaching that the author deems not only erroneous but pernicious. Jesus really came in the flesh, and to refuse to affirm this is heresy.

Historic and modern parallels and analogies are not far to seek. The definition of Jesus Christ's humanity has been and continues to be an important issue in Christology. His humanity is easily affirmed but in fact all too often lost, particularly in attempting to affirm and ensure that he is, to use classical theological language, truly God as well. Can he be both? The confession that he is indeed both has been the classical paradox of Christology. According to the logic of Christian soteriology (doctrine of salvation), Jesus Christ is irrelevant to the human condition if he is not truly human. On the other hand, he will be unable to bring salvation as relief from the human condition of sin and death if he is not at the same time truly God. In verse 2 Christ as life and eternal life is said to be "with the Father"; thus the Gospel (John 1:1) is clearly evoked, where we read that "the Word was with God, and the Word was God." Yet, as we have seen, 1 John's most urgent interest is reflected in the insistence upon Jesus' tangible humanity.

Early in the development of Christian doctrine emphasis was laid on Jesus' death. His death was the hallmark of his humanity, and his humanity was the necessary presupposition of his death. Through that death, salvation from sin was effected (1 Cor. 15:3; 1 John 2:2). Not surprisingly, toward the end of this letter John appears to underscore the importance of Jesus' death (5:6) in the face of those who overlook it.

Preaching from this text might well proceed along similar lines, for it affords an admirable basis for preaching on the incarnation. The fact that close examination suggests a controversy behind the text is really no impediment to preaching, for the kind of controversy we discover is directly related to a tension always present in Christology when it is being true to its biblical roots, namely, the tension between Christ's humanity and divinity. When that tension breaks down in either direction, orthodoxy is threatened and preaching becomes irrelevant or unreal.

Remarkably, the breakdown of that tension is a continuing

40

threat. Very often, exactly at the point or in quarters where Jesus' divinity is most strenuously extolled, the humanity that he shares with us is lost sight of or threatened. A kind of "Superman Christology" that refuses to contemplate a genuine humanity is as damaging to orthodoxy as its opposite. In such a Christology, Jesus' humanity becomes only an incognito behind which the true God is hidden. Jesus remains omnipotent and invulnerable, not really subject to the dangers that encompass or threaten us. But according to the New Testament, Jesus was truly human and, as such, subject to the same temptations and perils as we (Heb. 4:15). His humanity was no disguise. His death is eloquent testimony to this fact.

Another aspect of this text is relevant to the task of preaching generally, namely, its heavy emphasis upon the task of witness and proclamation (vv. 2–3). In the Common Lectionary reading, which continues through 2:2, this emphasis is picked up again in 1:5, where John speaks of the "message we have heard from him and proclaim to you," obviously the message of the gospel. The gospel is realized, actualized as gospel, precisely in the act of proclaiming it. In a quite real sense, this is a text *about* preaching as well as a text *for* preaching.

Thus although the Lectionary division of the text (1:1—2:2) appears to overlook the clear division between verses 4 and 5, it has its justification, for 1:5—2:2 elaborates the message about the coming, nature, and work of Jesus, and does so in a way quite typical of John. The division between light and darkness, found so frequently in the Johannine writings and elsewhere in the New Testament (e.g., 1 Cor. 4:5), appears here and is quickly given an ethical application or interpretation. Whether we walk in light or darkness has everything to do with how we live, particularly in relationship to others, as verses 6 and 7 clearly indicate. The possibility of walking in the light poses the opposite and alternative possibility, walking in darkness, that is, sin. Thus the atoning work of Christ, his dealing with sin, becomes the next theme of the letter. The atonement is, of course, an ancient and central aspect of the primitive Christian preaching (1 Cor. 15:3). Rather distinctively in the Johannine literature, incarnation and atonement are here linked. While 1:1–4 is a discrete unit, and we have treated it as such, the Lectionary division also makes sense, not only theologically, but against the background of the earliest history of Christian preaching.

41

1 John 1:5–10
The Message Heard and Proclaimed:
The Good News of Forgiveness

As we observed, the prologue (1:1–4) sets forth the incarnation of the word of life in a palpable, visible, human being whose name was Jesus. In this next section John speaks of the message that Jesus has brought and that he and his fellow preachers ("we") have proclaimed (v. 5). Initially, the message is described abstractly—"God is light"—but its more specific and concrete content is quickly spelled out. Typically, John refers immediately to the conduct of believers, how they walk (vv. 6–7), as he exhorts his readers to confess their sin. But in the background, and basic to his thought, is the atoning work of Christ, who cleanses the believer from sin, offering forgiveness, and thus life (vv. 7, 9). In a real sense 1:1–4 deals with the person of Christ, while this section treats his work, but in such a way that it cannot even be spoken of apart from the believer's response.

The gospel message presupposes the mortality, lostness, and sinfulness of human existence apart from God's revelation in Jesus. Without God's intervention we are going nowhere but remain locked in darkness (2:8–11) and death (3:14). Nowhere is 1 John's relationship to the Gospel of John clearer than in the perception of the hopelessness of the human plight as death and darkness apart from God's intervention (cf. John 3:16–21; 5:21–29; 11:25–26; on darkness 1:5; 9:39–41; 12:46). On the dire nature of this plight and the necessity of God's intervention, the Apostle Paul could not have agreed more (Rom. 3:21–26; 5:6–8).

That God is light (v. 5) means that God is freedom from darkness or death. To say that the gospel—good news—of God's salvation is the proclamation of God as light evokes the statement in the Gospel's prologue (1:5) that "the light shines in the darkness, and the darkness has not overcome it." It is also a clear allusion to the coming of Jesus as the light and life of humankind (John 1:4). The reader of the Gospel, ancient or modern, will know this—or learn it. Otherwise, to say that the message is that God is light and without any darkness sounds strangely abstract, but it is a proposition to which many people in the ancient world, pagan or Jewish, could easily have agreed. John's point is that in Jesus the light has shone in such a way as really to illumine human life.

Beginning with v. 6 the discussion takes a decidedly ethical and even practical turn. The imagery of darkness is continued, and the idea of fellowship (Greek: *koinōnia*) reappears. The claim to have fellowship with "him" (in this case, apparently God, although it could be Christ) is invalidated if one continues to walk in darkness (NRSV correctly: "are walking in darkness") and does not live according to the truth (NRSV, more literally: "do what is true"). Exactly how one walks in darkness or, for that matter, in light (v. 7) has not yet been clearly stated. If the reader looks ahead to verses 8 and 10, however, and notes their emphasis on the pervasiveness of sin, it is not difficult to guess that walking in darkness or light refers to one's conduct. This is confirmed by 2:9–11, where loving or hating one's fellow believer is the mark of walking in light or in darkness. Living "according to the truth" or doing what is true (v. 6) is walking in the light, for in the Johannine vocabulary the truth is Jesus himself, or, to spell it out fully, the revelation of God's reality in Jesus.

In verse 6 we see the first of a number of if-clauses typical of 1 John. "If we say" implies that someone is saying it (cf. 1:8, 10, etc.). There is in 1 John a recurring refrain on the possible tension between saying and doing. To speak correctly but not to act correctly is fundamentally suspect and specious. One's speaking must accord with one's actions, one's walking (2:6). Although 1 John never quotes the Old Testament (cf. 3:12 for the only reference), the metaphor of walking to refer to one's conduct or way of life is biblical and typically Jewish. Walking in the light as he (again God, but in principle possibly Jesus also) is in the light (v. 7) *means* having fellowship with one another and being cleansed from all sin by the blood of Jesus.

This does not mean that walking in the light is prior to, or a precondition of, such fellowship and cleansing. Rather Jesus' sacrificial death makes such walking and fellowship possible. Elsewhere John insists that the priority and initiative lie with God, not with human attitudes or conduct (4:10). The saving effect of Jesus' death lay at the heart of much early Christian preaching and theology, as the New Testament clearly shows (1 Cor. 15:3; Gal. 2:20–21; Rom. 3:21–26; 1 Peter 2:24). Moreover,

43

it is quite plain that Christ's death is conceived as a blood sacrifice (Mark 14:24; cf. 1 Cor. 11:25; Rom 3:25; Eph. 1:7; Heb. 9:11–14) and as such is to be understood against the background of the Old Testament sacrificial system. (Indeed, one of the major themes of the Letter to the Hebrews is that Christ's sacrifice in principle displaces that system.) We shall return to the subject of cultic sacrifice, but for the moment it suffices to observe that Jesus' death, a historical event in Jerusalem, the seat of the Temple, was understood by the earliest Christians as effective for salvation because it was a sacrifice on the analogy of the sacrifices of the Temple. Of course, the questions of who was sacrificed, by whom, and why were central issues for earliest Christian theology. Not any bloody human death, but specifically the death of Jesus, the Christ, God's only son (John 3:16), effects cleansing and salvation for humankind. By referring to Jesus' death here, 1 John underscores its importance, more so than the Fourth Gospel, in which the sacrificial aspects of Jesus' death are alluded to (cf. 1:29) but not developed.

Jesus' sacrifice for sin presupposes sin as pervasive, a malady characteristic of the human condition (cf. Rom. 3:21). To deny sin is to undercut the economy of salvation, not only by lying ourselves (v. 8) but by making God a liar (v. 10). Here in verse 10, as throughout this passage, the subject is God, although it could equally well be Christ, whose saving work would become unnecessary and vacuous apart from the pervasiveness of sin. The polarity or tension between truth and lie, which is an aspect of the Johannine dualism, now comes into play. Anyone who confesses his or her sin acknowledges the truth, but to deny one's sinfulness is to lie, and it is precisely that lie that prevents a person from receiving God's saving work.

Interestingly, some commentators have taken verses 8 and 10 to refer to sin committed before Christ's blood has cleansed us. In that case there would be no contradiction with statements later on that imply the true believer's sinlessness (cf. 3:4–10). Yet verse 9 refers to ongoing confession and forgiveness as a part of Christian life and worship, and 2:1 makes this meaning clear. When in 3:8 John says that the Son of God appeared to destroy the works of the devil, Wesley comments: "And will He not perform this in all that trust in Him?" The latter statement (3:8) occurs just before the author writes, "No one born of God commits sin" (3:9). There seems to be an unresolved tension in 1 John as there was in Wesley. On the one hand, Christ died for sin, so that its continued existence in the believer is unthinkable. Yet exist it does, even in the Christian, as 1:8 and 9 would seem to acknowledge (cf. 2:1). Nevertheless, in principle sin is conquered and must be rooted out. Neither John nor John Wesley is inclined to admit that it cannot be. Indeed, to strike a concordat with sin is to capitulate before it and to deny the effectiveness of Christ's work as decisively as if one refuses to acknowledge sin at all. Thus John (and Wesley following him) will speak of the perfection of love in the believer (2:5; 4:17, 18, 19), a theme that is unique to the Epistle, although in the Gospel Jesus speaks of the perfection or completion of unity among believers (17:23)—clearly a related idea. No New Testament writing manifests the tension between the reality of sin—even in believers—and the demand of Christ for perfection more dramatically than 1 John.

The two major aspects of John's teaching in this pericope—sacrifice and sin—reflect the doctrine and praxis of the earliest church while at the same time providing seminal scriptural grist for the theological mills of many later generations of Christians.

The idea of Christ's death as sacrifice on the cultic model, that is, blood sacrifice, is quite strange to modern, Western experience in a way it was not to ancient. Of course, Christians in parts of India and Africa may not be unfamiliar with the sacrificial practices that are presupposed. They may have seen, if not at one time participated in, animal sacrifice. Remarkably, many Christians in Western cultures seem to fall into the language of cultic sacrifice quite easily, perhaps because it is so much a part of our scripture and tradition. Of course, the sacrificial dimension of religion is also preserved in the Catholic understanding of the Eucharist as the re-presentation of the sacrifice of Christ.

Perhaps the ease with which we adopt such language is also related to the pervasiveness of sacrifice and particularly animal sacrifice (at an earlier stage human sacrifice) in the history of religion. Almost all our ancestors, whether in Eurasia, Africa, or the Americas, practiced animal sacrifice at one time. Why was the practice so widespread? Obviously not because people in prehistoric Mexico were influenced by the ancient Hebrews, or vice versa. Something about human existence, human consciousness of mortality and sin, calls forth the need to sacrifice,

45

to make reparation, to restore community with God. All of which is to say that the understanding of Christ's death as sacrifice for sin is not only biblically grounded but based on an aspect of human consciousness that is, or once was, almost universal. It is clear that transactions among people and with God do not go on at a purely intellectual level or in verbal communications only. What God demands is serious and real—in some sense it is our lives. According to the gospel, the life and blood of Jesus are offered for our lives, and that makes sense to us.

The concept of sacrifice thus answers to that of sin. Sin is a death-dealing breach of relationship with God that is murderous in its effect (3:11–15). Initially, John speaks of "sin" in the singular (1:7–8; cf. John 1:29), not of "sins" in the plural, although it quickly becomes clear that sin leads to sinning and to sins (1:9; 2:2). There is a root cause, sin, that leads to concrete expression. That sin is in the first place a condition rather than an infringement of a specific moral law is suggested by the fact that it can be paralleled by such ideas as walking in darkness (1:6), loving the world (2:15), not knowing the truth (2:21), lawlessness (3:4), and hating one's brother or sister (4:20). The condition of alienation from God and from one's fellows to which the gospel is addressed is what is meant by sin. Ultimately, sin is death (3:14), and there is no escape from it except the one God provides. That escape is accessible through the word of the gospel, which is the word about Jesus Christ.

All this sounds very much like the Apostle Paul, and, indeed, there is a remarkable similarity between the Pauline and Johannine views of sin. In each case sin as alienation or lostness characterizes the human situation, and Jesus Christ is the revelation of God's initiative and graciousness that means freedom from sin ("walking in the light"). Strangely, 1 John does not use the word *grace* (Greek: *charis*) that is so characteristic of Pauline theology (but cf. 2 John 3, where it appears in a salutation, and John 1:14, 16–17, the only instances in the Gospel). Perhaps this is as good an indication as we could have that John did not know Paul's letters, even though the substance of their thought is so similar. In any event, for both Paul and John sin is an unavoidable aspect of the givenness of the human situation to which God in the gospel speaks.

In preaching from such a text as this, one can scarcely avoid being drawn into the circle of traditional and historic Christian doctrine in which Christ's death is set forth as the answer to the problem of sin. There is a certain obviousness about the subject matter of 1 John 1:5–10, whether for teaching or preaching. In one of his instructional tapes, a well-known tennis professional advocates hitting the obvious shot and describes how much difficulty players make for themselves when they fail to do so. The analogy with preaching is clear enough. Just because countless preachers and their congregations have found in the preaching of Christ's sacrifice their deliverance and healing from sin, we should not be discouraged from preaching on these themes today! Preaching needs to be original in presentation but not in its basic themes. Obviously these notes can be struck in such a way as to seem perfunctory, but the relating of the biblical perception of the human condition and the gospel to specific aspects of human lostness and entrapment and to the nature and possibilities of redemption is ever an exciting and challenging task.

One caveat is worth issuing in view of a common habit of Christian preaching, both ancient and modern. In order to make the gospel persuasive, it has often been thought necessary first to prove that humanity is, indeed, lost in sin. Paul's Letter to the Romans could be read in this way, with 1:18—3:20 understood as Paul's (or God's) indictment of human sinfulness. This is not an erroneous reading so long as one remembers that it is genuinely Paul's perception of the human situation apart from Christ. Yet it is also an assessment of that situation based on the gospel, so that Paul seems to move theologically from solution to plight. There is a large element of truth in this insight, which has been advanced or supported by influential modern interpreters. Nevertheless, such a description of the human condition, whether in Paul or John, would have no convincing power if it did not, so to speak, ring a bell—if people did not see in it an accurate perception of what they had already sensed about their own lives and the society in which they live. Yet once it is felt to be necessary to prove a point about human sinfulness, something essential is lost. That condition cannot really be proven; it can at most be appealed to in the expectation that the assumption or description of human sinfulness will strike a familiar chord. To attempt to prove it makes preaching strident and tiresome.

47

John Wesley, along with many other preachers through the centuries, thought it necessary and proper to begin to address a congregation not with a condemnation of human sinfulness but with a statement of God's grace. Against the backdrop of God's gracious goodness, human sinfulness stands out clearly. Only then can it be seen for what it is, although its reality may already be felt or sensed. In 1 John we see the beginning of this way of proceeding (as in Rom. 1:16–17): First, the good news is announced (1:5; cf. 1:1–4); then the reality of human sinfulness is juxtaposed to it. Christ as answer allows the lineaments of the human question to come into clear focus.

REFLECTION:
The Language of 1 John

A common vocabulary within a common language, whether English or Greek, often marks off a distinct social group, whether theological, religious, or political. As we have already observed, 1 John shows the vocabulary of sin and salvation common to other early Christians, yet the choice of language in 1 John (and the other two letters) is reminiscent of nothing so much as the Gospel of John. We have now come far enough in 1 John to see firsthand the extent to which this is the case. After the initial reference to the beginning *(archē)* in each prologue, the most obvious parallel is perhaps the identification of Jesus as the word *(logos)* in 1 John 1:1 and John 1:14. Of course, were it not for the Gospel, it would not be so obvious to us that "the word of life" in 1 John 1:1 is Jesus Christ. Strikingly, only in the prologue of each is the *logos* to be identified with Jesus. Otherwise, *logos* occurs in both, but of the spoken word only, which is its most common meaning in the New Testament.

The history and usage of *logos* and related terms and concepts is conveniently set out in the article on *legō* (to speak), *logos,* etc., in the *Theological Dictionary of the New Testament* (vol. IV, pp. 69–192), the work of a number of scholars, experts in Old Testament or New Although Kittel, as it is called after its founder and editor Gerhard Kittel, has been roundly criticized for methodological unclarity (for example, in mixing philology with theology and the analysis of specific terms with more general concepts), it remains a valuable repository of information on New Testament vocabulary and conceptuality.

48

The work was conceived in Germany long before World War II and was begun, logically enough, at the beginning of the Greek alphabet. After the war, and Kittel's death, it continued under the direction of his successor Gerhard Friedrich, taking up at the Greek letter *xi* with volume V. Now a new generation of German scholars began to contribute. Before it was completed, an English translation was begun under the direction of Geoffrey W. Bromiley (1964). That translation has been complete for some years (since 1976), and a shorter, one-volume English version has now been produced that has been made accessible to readers who do not use Greek. The postwar contributors could take advantage of such archaeological discoveries as the Dead Sea Scrolls. In vocabulary and theological concepts the newly discovered writings in this cache of documents bear a remarkable resemblance to the New Testament, particularly to the Johannine literature. The Hebrew equivalents of such terms as "life," "light," and "truth" are prominent in the Scrolls.

In the prologue of 1 John, as well as in the Gospel, the word *(logos)* is identified with life (*zōē;* cf. 1 John 1:2; John 1:4), again a typically Johannine term. *Zōē* was studied by Rudolf Bultmann in Kittel (*TDNT,* vol. II, pp. 832–875). Bultmann, the most famous German New Testament scholar of the twentieth century, wrote a monumental commentary on the Gospel of John (English title: *The Gospel of John: A Commentary*), as well as a commentary on the Epistles. Not coincidentally, Bultmann had been commissioned to write several important Kittel articles on typically Johannine terms. Thus he also wrote the article on *alētheia* ("truth," vol. I, pp. 233–251). Interestingly enough, already in 1 John 1:6 we encounter the odd expression "to do the truth" (cf. also John 3:21), which is paralleled in the Scrolls (*Manual of Discipline* 1:5; 5:3; 8:2), a fact Bultmann could not have known when he wrote the article. Bultmann identified the background and meaning of Johannine vocabulary as Gnostic, or derived from the religious movement or ideology we know as Gnosticism. This was an understandable move since many terms common to the Gospel and Epistle of John were used by Gnostic Christians—not only "word," "truth," and "life," but "light," "darkness," and "world," not to mention the verb "to know," *ginōskein,* from which *Gnosticism* is derived. Bultmann had also written the article on *ginōskō* (*TDNT,* vol. I, pp. 689–719).

49

Again, after World War II a large number of ancient Gnostic documents were discovered at Nag Hammadi in Upper Egypt, which confirmed that the language the orthodox Christian Fathers attributed to Gnostics was, in fact, used by them (and, incidentally, that it was remarkably similar to the Johannine vocabulary). These documents were, however, second century or later, whereas the Dead Sea Scrolls could be dated with certainty to the century prior to the origin of Christianity, if not before. The debate over whether Gnosticism was earlier than Christianity has not been settled by this discovery.

Meanwhile, the discovery of the Scrolls demonstrated that many of the key terms and concepts of the Johannine vocabulary were not only used by, but apparently had great significance for, some pre-Christian, Palestinian Jews. Bultmann's view that the vocabulary and theology of John had roots in Gnosticism was thus commonly said to be disproved. Bultmann, however, felt that his position had rather been confirmed, for he saw in the Scrolls a distinctly Jewish Gnosticism. (Indeed, he had already hypothesized an oriental—Palestinian or Syrian—Gnosticism as the background of the Fourth Gospel.) Certainly some of the Scrolls, especially the *Manual of Discipline,* manifest a dualism (light versus the darkness, truth versus the lie) similar to what is found in Gnosticism and in the Johannine writings, as well as the affinities of vocabulary already mentioned. But the kind of redeemer myth posited by Bultmann, which would have provided the model for New Testament Christology, is nowhere to be seen. The close kinship between the dualism of John and the Scrolls, with the related affinities in vocabulary, has been studied by James H. Charlesworth in an important article on that subject (originally published in *New Testament Studies* but now perhaps most easily available in the volume *John and the Dead Sea Scrolls,* edited by Charlesworth.)

Whatever the origin of the Johannine vocabulary, it has strong Jewish roots, as the Scrolls attest. At the same time the affinities with Gnosticism are significant, however they may be explained. Moreover, as we have noted, an unmistakably close kinship in vocabulary, and hence theological conceptuality, binds the Gospel and Epistles of John together. If they are not from the same author, they are surely from the same circles of early Christianity (see my *Johannine Christianity*), if not from the same school (cf. R. Alan Culpepper, *The Johannine*

50

School). Over against the rest of the New Testament, the Johannine vocabulary is distinct without being unique. For example, the term for truth *(alētheia)* has nearly half of its New Testament occurrences (45 of 109) in the relatively brief compass of the Gospel and letters of John. Something similar is true of the term *kosmos,* "world" (102 of 186) and the verb *ginōskein,* "to know" (83 of 222). John's language is, by and large, found elsewhere in the New Testament: It is the Johannine emphasis that stands out. Nearly a century ago (1905), E. A. Abbott published a comprehensive study, *Johannine Vocabulary.* Since then, although there have been numerous specific and specialized studies, there has been no comparable general treatment. A useful, compact study may, however, be consulted in Brown's commentary, *The Gospel According to John,* vol. I (1966), pp. 497–518. A consideration of Johannine vocabulary is essential to Johannine theology, and Brown's essay will prove rewarding even to the reader who does not use Greek.

1 John 2:1–6
Walking in the Way He Walked: Obedience and Knowledge of Christ

John addresses his readers and again refers to the fact that he is writing (2:1; cf. 1:4). This marks a new segment of his discussion; hence in the RSV a new paragraph begins. The address to "my little children" may well have a specific church or circle of Christians for whom he has responsibility in view. (In John 13:33 Jesus refers to his disciples with the same word, *teknia.*) Nevertheless, the commentators who see here an address to all Christians (see Introduction) are not necessarily wrong. In fact, through the centuries the author has spoken to more readers and hearers than he could have imagined.

As is typical of 1 John, this section begins with a statement about the work of Christ and ends with an ethical exhortation. The purpose of writing is, however, hortatory, "that you may not sin" (v. 1). This purpose then leads to reflection on the work of Christ. Again sacrificial terminology appears; Jesus is the

51

"expiation" (Greek: *hylasmos;* cf. *hylastērion* in Rom. 3:25) for sin, not only for Christians, but potentially for the whole world (v. 2). Quite obviously, in light of the possibility of believers' sinning and their need for expiation, a sacrificial dealing with sin through Jesus' death is in view. (The NRSV translates "atoning sacrifice" instead of "expiation.") All this makes good sense to us today and accords with two millennia of Christian experience: Christians also sin and need to confess their sins and repent in the assurance of forgiveness (1:8–10).

The terms in which Jesus Christ and his work are described are significant. He is said to be our advocate with God the Father, and he is called righteous (Greek: *dikaios*). "Advocate" translates the same Greek word, *paraklētos,* that is used of the Holy Spirit in the farewell discourses of the Gospel. In fact, when the term is first used (John 14:16), the Spirit is called "another *paraklētos.*" The RSV translates "Counselor" there and throughout the Gospel, but "advocate" here. (The NRSV returns to "Advocate" in the Gospel.) The latter is closer to the literal meaning of the word, which is "one called to the side of." It can be used to refer to an attorney. That original meaning fits 1 John better than the Gospel, for here Jesus Christ after his sacrificial death and exaltation to heaven intercedes before God for us all.

Jesus is also called righteous *(dikaios),* an allusion to the description of Jesus just preceding (1:9) as one who is faithful and just *(dikaios)* to forgive and cleanse us. While the term "advocate" *(paraklētos)* is distinctly Johannine, to say that Jesus is faithful and just or righteous is to describe him in terms that have a Pauline ring. At this point, as John describes Christ and his sacrificial work for us, he naturally uses traditional language, wherever he may have learned it. The description of Jesus as righteous probably echoes John 17:25, where Jesus addresses God as righteous in the conclusion of his prayer. To call Jesus "righteous" (cf. Acts 3:14; 7:52) is to suggest something about what his followers should be (1 John 3:7) and foreshadows what is to be said about keeping his commandments (2:3–6).

The very simple statement about being sure that we know Jesus, or knowing that we know him (v. 3), introduces a new element or theme, the knowledge of Christ and thus of God. Some form of the verb "to know" appears quite often in the Gospel of John and 1 John, even more frequently than in other New Testament books, where it is also rather common. Knowledge of God and Christ is then a major and distinctive theme of the Johannine literature. In 1 John, and perhaps also in the Gospel, the emphasis on knowledge is motivated by a need for reassurance, or to afford reassurance, and thus answers the implied question, "How may we be sure we know him?"

Yet the reassurance sought and given is not just a matter of receiving and believing testimony about what has happened, as important as that may be. There is a kind of existential reassurance that comes only when the testimony believed is acted upon. Thus one is sure that one knows Jesus in obeying his commandments. The Gospel puts it somewhat differently: "Anyone who resolves to do the will of God will know whether the teaching is from God or whether I am speaking on my own" (John 7:17, NRSV). But the basic understanding is the same. The genuine intention, the will, determines and reveals one's true belief. In 1 John this train of thought would seem to be developed further. One's will ultimately becomes manifest in what is actually done: "But if any one has the world's goods and sees his brother in need, yet closes his heart against him, how does God's love abide in him? Little children, let us not love in word or speech but in deed and in truth" (3:17–18; cf. Jesus' word in Matt. 7:20). While it is clear already from the Gospel that actual obedience to Christ's commandments is the only sure key to fellowship with him (John 14:15–17, 21, 23–24), in 1 John this is spelled out in quite concrete and specific terms.

In emphasizing the positive side of what John writes, we should not overlook the negative. To claim to know Jesus without obeying him involves one not only in a specious claim but a heinous lie (v. 4). This is the worst kind of denial of Christ, and against this sort of heinousness, John directs his sharpest attack. After thus underscoring the outrageousness of all false claims to know Christ, John reiterates the positive side (v. 5) and in doing so reassures the faithful reader who obeys Jesus' command or keeps his word (the two expressions are synonymous) of his or her true and secure status.

At this point it is worth recalling that in the Gospel the commandments of Christ boil down to the commandment to love (13:34; 15:12). Although Jesus speaks of commandments (plural), the only commandment he specifies is the commandment to love. The same would seem to be the case in 1 John, for in the next paragraph the author switches to the singular as he plays upon the old and new commandment (2:7–11), which

53

is obviously the commandment to love, as 3:11 shows (cf. 3:16 and John 15:12–13). To know Jesus Christ then is to live in love with one's fellow believers, to walk in the light. As we shall see, to hate is to remain in darkness (2:9, 11).

When John writes about the one who says she or he abides in Jesus walking in the same way Jesus walked (v. 6), he means, of course, walking in love. (On the imagery of walking, see below, p. 144.) One should not read this statement as if the "ought to walk" were somehow an option (cf. John 13:14). Such walking is the only possible demonstration of abiding in him, the authentic language of Christian obedience and confession. At the same time, it functions as the obedient believer's ultimate reassurance. Are you unsure whether or not you know Jesus Christ? Well, are you obeying his commandment? Are you walking as he walked? Walking as Jesus walked means loving unconditionally and without limitation. The only limit is that imposed by our finitude and death, but even death may become the definitive and ultimate expression of that love (3:16; John 15:12–13).

This text is a rich source of Christian teaching. The initial statements (2:1–2) hark back to 1:7–10 and take up the theme of the saving work of Christ, who is the advocate of the believer before God. That Christ is presently alive and at work is a central aspect, often a presumption, of New Testament Christology. The risen Jesus is and was and is to come (Rev. 1:4), and it is not by chance that the seer of Revelation refers first to his present activity—he is. Thus prayers are addressed to Jesus as to God (1 Cor. 16:22; Rev. 22:20; 2 Cor. 12:8; Acts 7:59–60). Such prayers doubtless sound a bit odd to many people brought up in modern, mainline Protestant Christianity, for whom Jesus is a great figure looming up out of the past but scarcely a force to be reckoned with in the present. For Catholic and Pentecostal Christianity, however, the presence of Christ is a familiar reality, whether because of the eucharistic liturgy or some more spontaneous expression. Jesus is now; he is not just back there, out there, or expected somehow in the more-or-less distant future. He lives and rules.

The turn taken in 2:3–6 initiates another train of thought. John indicates quite simply and plainly that theology and ethics must not be divorced; that is, true faith finds expression in good works. A more Johannine formulation would be: Right confes-

54

sion of Jesus is tested by obedience to him. Modern theologians have talked, in a shorthand way, about the *indicative* and the *imperative*. That is, what God has done (indicative) lays the basis for us to act in response (imperative). There is no firmer scriptural basis for such a distinction than 1 John. But notice how John can look at matters from the other, human end, so to speak. Not that obedience is prior to confession, or works to faith, but obedience in faithful works is very much allowed, and insisted upon, as the verification or test of true faith. This is not said in a threatening mode but rather to reassure the readers, perhaps originally in the face of those who would attempt to unsettle their faith by appeal to other extrinsic criteria (such as secret wisdom or knowledge or esoteric experience). We do not know precisely the source or nature of this threat, but the repeated efforts of John to reassure his readers on the trustworthiness of right confession and conduct and the allusions to those who do not confess or conduct themselves properly indicate the reality of such opposition.

The Common Lectionary division of this text, between 2:2 and 3 makes good sense, particularly for preaching. It leaves the first two verses of the chapter with 1:5–10; this is appropriate, for they continue the theme of the work of Christ in dealing with sin. In 1:7 Christ's death on the cross is primarily in view, and in 2:1 his present heavenly intercession, but the two are intimately related theologically. On the other hand, if we begin with 1:5 and go down through 2:6, there is a nice symmetry or even chiastic structure of the pericope. First, John deals with ethics or obedience, walking in light or darkness (1:5–7a); then with sin and the atoning and intercessory work of Christ (1:7b—2:2), on earth (1:7) and in heaven (2:1); finally, he returns to deal with ethics or obedience again, keeping Jesus' commandments and walking as he walks (2:3–6). Although there is scarcely a logical progression through the entire section, taken as a whole its integrity and meaning are real and relevant. Perhaps it would be difficult to deal with every aspect of such a pericope (1:5—2:6) in one sermon, but the integral relationship between theology and ethics, faith and action, is worth preserving.

Another important aspect of this text, and one that deserves close attention in preaching, is the element of reassurance present in 2:3–6. This is a central and underlying theme of the letter, one that deserves emphasis and underscoring in our day as in John's. In part Christian preaching appeals to the intrinsic precariousness and fragility of human existence, a state of affairs that dominates or threatens the consciousness of many people. As Jesus promises to "deliver all those who through fear of death were subject to lifelong bondage" (Heb. 2:15), this appeal is not misplaced. Yet it is easily deflected, so that this precariousness and the character of reassurance are misunderstood.

The Christian message rightly directs itself to human uncertainty and vulnerability before the vicissitudes of life and death, and is correctly understood as offering assurance and hope. In 1 John we encounter an important insight about how that assurance, or reassurance, can be attained and authenticated. Not by some spiritual experience or esoteric knowledge is that reassurance given, but by walking in the light as he (God) is in the light or by walking in the same way in which he (Jesus) walked. Neither theological knowledge nor spiritual experience afford valid reassurance apart from walking after Jesus in the light. The images of walking and light have to do with conduct and particularly with human relationships. In the community or fellowship of believers true light and love are found. Their presence is the Christian's reassurance in both giving and receiving. Their presence is intrinsically reassuring, and in the presence of doubt or despair they can be pointed to as evidence of the reality in which faith believes.

1 John 2:7–11
The Old and New Commandments: A Fundamental Teaching

Once again John begins a new phase of his discussion by indicating that he is writing, this time to readers he describes as "beloved" (2:7). In doing so he may evoke the memory of the disciple whom Jesus loved, the Beloved Disciple of the Gospel of John (John 13:23; 19:26; 20:2; 21:7, 20), who is otherwise not mentioned in the Epistles in John. But the term "beloved" in the Greek vocative plural form *(agapētoi)* is not uncommon in other New Testament letters (e.g., Rom. 12:19; Heb. 6:9; 1 Peter 2:11) and can be rendered "dear friends." Quite possibly

John addressed a specific Christian community, or communities, but his "beloved" can easily be extended to the whole Christian church or to all who hear his words gladly. Christians have traditionally read it in this way.

He writes now about a commandment that is not unfamiliar. Those whom he addresses already know about this commandment; it is not new but old. Similarly, the reader, whether ancient or modern, who knows the Gospel of John will know this commandment (John 13:34; 15:12). In the Gospel, of course, it is described as new, and from the perspective of Jesus it is new. John means, of course, Jesus' commandment to love one another. That the commandment should be known from the Gospel as the new commandment sheds light on John's manner of speaking here, for he writes as if he and his readers know that Gospel. That they have had the old commandment from the beginning means that they have had it from the beginning of the tradition and community, and this is a veiled way of saying they have it from Jesus. (The NRSV correctly translates the imperfect tense of 2:7 "have had," giving it its proper continuative force.) The ancient reader would have understood this, and the contemporary reader familiar with the Gospel will know it as well. Moreover, this understanding of "beginning" supports our interpretation of "that which was from the beginning" in 1:1 as really referring to Jesus himself.

The author does not yet say that he is speaking of the love commandment, but evidently the readers will know that he is. Not only does he refer to it as the commandment to love in 3:11, but what he writes in 2:9–11 makes good sense only if he has the love commandment in view here as well. The equation of commandment or word (2:7) and message is obvious enough.

That Jesus commanded his followers to love their fellow believers represents a particularly Johannine slant (John 13:34; 1 John 3:11). Jesus' command to love is found at other points in the New Testament but with a somewhat different emphasis. In the synoptic story of the good scribe who asks Jesus about the first (most important) commandment (Mark 12:28–34), Jesus responds with the Shema—love of God (cf. Deut. 6:4)—and then with the command to love one's neighbor (cf. Lev. 19:18). At least this second commandment seems to be known to Paul, who twice refers to it (Rom. 13:9; Gal. 5:14) and in both instances says that love is the fulfilling of the law, although in neither case does he attribute the command to Jesus. Perhaps

57

everyone would have known its origin. According to the synoptic tradition, Jesus also commanded love of enemy (Matt. 5:44; Luke 6:27), and this command may also be reflected by Paul (Rom. 12:17–21). Thus Jesus seems deliberately to have removed any limits or restrictions on love.

For John also love is to be limitless, in the sense that it may require the surrendering of one's own life (John 15:12–13; 1 John 3:16). Yet in another dimension it is quite limited to, or focused upon, the disciples or the Johannine community. Even in Jesus' promulgation of the commandment, he tells his disciples to love one another (John 13:34; 15:12), and our epistle takes up this restrictive focus in its language about loving one's brother (2:9–11 and throughout the letter). That men and women are included under *adelphoi*, brothers, may be assumed. The use of the masculine gender says something about the character of the Greek language but scarcely bespeaks any gender-defined limitation of love! To make the point plain, the NRSV consistently translates *adelphoi* "brother or sister" (or the like) and makes similar adjustments to correspond with contemporary usage. (Thus in 2:6, 9, 10, and 11, "he who" becomes "whoever.")

This seeming restriction of the command to love is a problem for Johannine interpretation, in that we wonder how to construe or apply it in our own lives and situations, but John's meaning seems to be clear enough. It may be that John does not intend to restrict love to the beloved community, or church, but we cannot deny that his language, and apparently his intention, concentrates the command of Jesus on that community. In 2:15–17 love of the world is forbidden to the believer, but that does not necessarily mean that persons in the world and still bound to the world are not to be loved. Nevertheless, love of the neighbor, much less of the enemy, is not enjoined, and in the Johannine letters the Gospel's affirmation that God in the sending of his Son loved the world (John 3:16) is at least muted (1 John 4:9).

John's rather narrow focus upon love among believers is probably related to the community's and the author's sense of isolation in a hostile environment. The source of the hostility is characterized in the Gospel not only as "the world" but also as "the Jews." The Christians addressed by the Gospel have apparently been expelled from the synagogue as the culmination of internecine strife over the question of the messiahship of Jesus.

This state of affairs is, however, nowhere in evidence in the letters. Here the opposition and tension, so extreme that John characterizes his opponents as antichrists (2:18), is within the church, within the community of those who confess Jesus as the Christ. Their dispute seems to be centered upon what that confession means, with regard both to the nature of Christ (Christology) and to the nature of discipleship. Occasionally John throws out hints that these opponents have become very numerous and influential indeed (4:5). In such a situation, John's concentration upon love among the brethren, love within the community for the sake of its fellowship (1:4), and unity (cf. John 17:20–26) is understandable. Love for those outside the disciples, or church, is not in principle excluded, but love among those who are on the inside takes priority. In the Gospel at least this love should be a witness to all humanity (13:35), but this is not so explicitly stated in 1 John.

John takes up the term "new commandment" found in the Gospel and interprets its newness. In the Gospel that newness had a temporal significance; the command to love was new in the sense of novel or only now promulgated. Now that signification is no longer valid; temporally speaking the commandment has become old. Yet it can still be called new, for it belongs to the new age of God's reign that has appeared with Jesus. This new age is light (because the light shines in darkness; John 1:5) and the new commandment typifies this light. It is light for seeing, walking, and living. The person who follows the love commandment of Jesus, who then follows Jesus (1 John 2:6), sees, lives, and walks by the light of God's reign, of God's new age that is breaking into the darkness of this old world. By the same token, all who refuse this light consign themselves to continued darkness, in which they will surely stumble (2:10–11).

Interestingly enough, the eschatology of 1 John, that is, the concept of the unfolding of history toward its end, seems in some significant ways closer to the synoptic tradition, Jesus, and Paul than to the Fourth Gospel. The Jesus of the Synoptic Gospels, along with Paul, looks forward to the arrival of God's kingdom in the future. In 1 John we learn that this new age is breaking into this old world, but not without struggle. Already the apocalyptic figure of the Antichrist appears (2:18). Probably 1 John is in this respect closer to Paul, who also saw signs of the advent of God's new age in the present (cf. Rom. 13:11–13), than to any other major New Testament witness. Yet the First

59

Epistle also shares with the Gospel of John the sense that the expected end time is already attaining fulfillment.

As we have seen, this text deals with a basic element of Christian teaching, the love commandment, that is widely represented and reflected in the New Testament. Both in the Synoptic Gospels and in John it is attributed to Jesus himself. In all probability it did originate with him, whether or not the formulations we now have are his. Significantly, both in the Jesus tradition of the Synoptics and in Paul the formulation is obviously drawn from Leviticus 19:18, and the commandment is taken to epitomize the teaching of the law. Although Paul does not attribute it to Jesus, it is hard to say how it could have attained its present prominence had he not been associated with it. Thus the love commandment appears initially among Jesus' earliest disciples as a summation of the law. With good reason it has also attained in the popular mind the status of the essence of Jesus' own teaching, and quite happily so, for in all probability it was just that. Yet its deep biblical roots are real, and the reader should not lose sight of them.

To say that Jesus taught us to love, and that his love commandment is rightly enshrined in the center of the New Testament, is true enough, and very significant indeed. Yet the invocation of love per se has not proven to be the solution to every ethical problem or dilemma, as the history of Christian exegesis and ethics amply demonstrates. Already in the Johannine literature the problematic aspects of the love commandment come into view, perhaps precisely because its importance and centrality are insisted upon so strongly.

John takes up and amplifies Jesus' love command but at the same time focuses and limits it quite sharply. We have already observed that his limitation of it is in some important sense an expression or reflection of a hostile environment. A striking corollary of this is the fact that the verb "to hate" occurs more frequently in the Gospel of John than in any other Gospel, and more frequently in 1 John than in any other letter, the Book of Acts, or Revelation! Of course, hatred is nowhere approved or enjoined. Rather, the disciples of Jesus and his church are going to be, or already are, the *objects* of hatred, particularly hatred by the world. Somewhat surprisingly, the Gospel of John does not speak directly of the Jews as hating Jesus, although they are likely included in the world's hatred, which is profound (John

15:18–19; 1 John 3:13). In 1 John the world includes just about everyone outside the community of disciples or the church. Yet the opponents within, that is, opponents who profess belief, are also viewed as making common cause with the world because they are of the world (4:5). The world finds them attractive and listens to them. Thus their very success confirms their worldliness. One has the impression of a sea of hatred in which the Johannine community exists as an island of love, beleaguered and even betrayed. In the very nature of the case, love must be focused inward, for outside the community it is rejected. Yet at least for the author of the Gospel the expression of this love, which undergirds the unity of the church, becomes a witness to the world (John 13:35; 17:21, 23)—a point well worth our attention.

Perhaps not surprisingly, in 1 John it is evident that there are those within the church whose attitude toward their fellows is marked by hatred rather than love (2:9, 11; 3:15; 4:20). Although John never identifies these folk explicitly, he probably has his opponents in view; quite likely they are the antichrists (2:18) or false prophets (4:1) who espouse false doctrine. While we read John's opinion of them, whoever they may have been, we do not hear their opinion of him and of his followers. Is the exclusion of love of enemies related to the hard line that John takes? Quite possibly so. Most Christian readers will naturally side with the canonical writers, or at least give them the benefit of the doubt. Moreover, what John says here about loving and hating is certainly true in principle. Nevertheless, it is evident that John is unwilling to give his opponents the benefit of the doubt, but rather makes use of his fundamentally dualistic conceptuality to dispose of them as existing within the realm of the lie, darkness, death, and the world. They are, so to speak, beyond the pale. Such dismissal of heretics and opponents is characteristic of the Catholic Epistles and of much of the post-apostolic Christian literature. The problem is the relative weight of the claims of truth and of love.

In preaching from this pericope it will be natural to deal with the love commandment, which is, of course, a central aspect of Christian teaching. There are, on the other hand, places in the New Testament where Jesus' command to love is set forth in a more straightforward way. What John is here talking about requires some explanation. Yet the explaining is

61

likely to be worth the trouble, for the dialectic between old and new affords opportunity to explore essential aspects or dimensions of the Christian message. The oldness of the love commandment underscores the importance of origins, especially Jesus (who draws upon the scriptures of Israel) as the fountainhead of Christian tradition and teaching. The Christian faith has an essential historical dimension or component; its past is authoritative. At the same time, faith looks to the future, for the future belongs to God. It is already God's rule and reign, characterized by the new commandment of love, which is true (i.e., real) in Jesus and in the believer. That is, in Jesus and in the community of believers ("you" is plural in Greek) the truth of God's love is realized. Whether that love exists or not is the clue and key to whether and where God's new age is coming into being. Thus God's plan for the future, for humanity, finds its fulfillment and realization only as people obey Jesus' commandment and walk in light rather than darkness.

As one preaches about love, it will be worthwhile to reflect on some tensions implicit in the perspectives that have already been suggested by 1 John. Is love to be limited to the community in which it is reciprocated or mutually shared? What about loving the unlovely, those who do not return our love or those who think and act in ways we disapprove? John's commandment of love, to love the brother and sister or love one another, stands in some tension with Jesus' command to love one's neighbor or even one's enemies. This is not so much a contradiction as it is a fruitful tension that should drive us to thoughtful reflection and meditation.

1 John 2:12–17
I Am Writing to You:
Do Not Love the World

The theme of this section is the polarity or hostility between God and the world, a recurring motif of 1 John. There does seem to be a break in the continuity between verses 14 and 15, as indicated by the paragraphing of the RSV and NRSV, but to isolate the two paragraphs leaves the several addresses to the various age groups hanging. "I am writing to you," says John, "because . . . ," and a reason is given for why he addresses each group. Yet nothing is yet said about the message that John wants to convey. It is quite possible, however, to see that message in verses 15–17, the strong warning against the world and worldliness. Although each of the groups (fathers, young men, children) is addressed in a complimentary way, the admonition in 2:15–17 if directed to all of them is not inappropriate. At one level the compliments then become a rhetorical device (a kind of *captivo benevolentiae*) to attract their favorable attention.

John uses the present tense in verses 12 and 13 to refer to his writing but the past (aorist) in verse 14. RSV translates "I am writing" in the one case and "I write" in the other. In verse 14 "I wrote" would be the more obvious translation of the Greek, although "I write" (epistolary aorist) is also quite correct. Probably the change is merely stylistic, and one need not postulate a previous writing or document.

Another problem is the translation of the word rendered "because" (RSV, followed by NRSV), which occurs in every clause, a total of six times. Most commentators prefer the translation "because," although that is not the only one possible. The Greek word *(hoti)* could be rendered "that," and the statements would have a somewhat different meaning: "I am writing to you, little children, that your sins are forgiven." One recent commentator (Raymond E. Brown) does not translate the *hoti* at all but understands it as a colon, denoting that what is (or has been) written is going to be cited: "I am writing to you children: your sins are forgiven." But if, as we suggest, the statements of verses 12–14 should lead into the exhortation of verses 15–17, the translation "because" fits well. Only those whose sins are forgiven, who know Jesus and the Father, who have overcome the evil one, who are strong and have the word of God abiding in them, are able to refuse the love of the world. Otherwise, it would be futile to exhort them to do so.

Interpreters have asked whether John is addressing actual age groups in verses 12–14, or whether church offices or some different categories of Christians are in view. Probably the simplest answer is the best: He is addressing different age groups. What he says to each is appropriate to them as such. John uses two different Greek words for children in verses 12 and 13 (NRSV, v. 14), but perhaps not too much should be made of this. (The RSV and NRSV distinguish them by translating *teknia* "little children" and *paidia* "children.") He uses different words also in 2:1 and 18, but in each case seems to be addressing all those to whom he is writing. Quite possibly in verse 12 he addresses the whole congregation also ("little children"); certainly all Christians are those whose sins are forgiven. Perhaps the familial form of address puts him in mind of other age groups.

Next, fathers are addressed (v. 13), and what is said about them is fitting, as once again we have a reference to the beginning. Apparently, the one "who was from the beginning" is Jesus himself. We have noticed that it is not unusual for Jesus to be described in this rather mysterious way. Obviously, John refers here to spiritual fathers (as Wesley noticed) and does not exclude women, but his language is influenced by the culture of which he is a part. His choice of *father* (v. 13) is probably influenced also by his application of the term to God. Whether this description of fathers is to be pressed historically—the fathers knew Jesus personally—is an unanswerable question. More than likely they did not but are representative of the generation contemporary with Jesus.

The young men (vv. 13, 14) are aptly and appropriately described also. Their youthful virility has conquered the evil one, presumably Satan, or perhaps his emissary the Antichrist (2:18; 4:3). In an obvious effort to be more inclusive, the NRSV translates *neaniskoi* "young people" rather than "young men;" but the specific contrast with "fathers" is then weakened. The word of God (v. 14) may be Christ himself (cf. John 1:1; Rev. 19:13), or it may be the commandment to love, which, coming from Christ, is the word of God. The two are not unrelated. Only in Revelation is Jesus referred to as the word of God; in the prologue of the Gospel he is simply the Word, and in the Epistle the word of life. Another emphasis shared with Revelation is the theme of conquering. Characteristically, 1 John speaks of conquering the evil one or the world (5:4), but Revelation frequently uses a participial form that the RSV translates "he who conquers," with no object. At the end of the farewell discourses of the Gospel, Jesus tells his disciples that he has overcome the world; 16:33 has the same Greek word, *nikan*. Clearly, the idea of conquering as a way of describing the Christian's relationship to the world is Johannine and ties Gospel, Epistle, and Revelation together. (The NRSV properly translates *nikan* "conquer," rather than "overcome" as in the RSV.)

In its context the reference to children in verse 13 must include those who are physically, in terms of age, actually children, although John could not lose sight of the fact that he also uses the term for all Christians (cf. v. 18). Again what is said of children here, like what is said in verse 12 of "little children," is also appropriate to all believers. "You know [or "have known"] the Father." Also with the mention of children, the idea of fatherhood, and hence God the Father, comes into play. It is noteworthy that what is said of the other age groups is appropriate to them only, but what is said about children could be applied to all Christians.

After this elaborate and somewhat repetitive address, John issues his famous warning against the world and worldliness. While a more explicit connection between verses 12–14 and verses 15–17, as well as between verses 17 and 18, might have been expected, the intrinsic relationship is real enough. The repeated addresses in verses 12–14 must lead somewhere. Moreover, one would expect the warnings against the world to be elaborated. In fact, both conditions are met. The rather elaborate words of address lead to a strong warning against worldliness. This is then followed by John's instancing of the attempted incursions of the world into the beloved community. Such incursion is represented preeminently by the opponents, who are mentioned immediately hereafter (2:18) and reappear later on (4:1), as John explicitly links them to the hostile world (4:4–5). In both cases they are called, or linked to, the Antichrist (2:18; 4:3).

John's condemnation of worldliness (vv. 15–17) is the Magna Carta of a certain kind of Christian pietism. Probably most Christian readers of this text have at some point shared in such a pietistic interpretation, even if they now distance themselves from it. A traditional, largely Protestant, puritanical piety has seen here a strong warning against things such as card playing, the cinema, dancing, smoking, or drinking. In other words, anything that affords sensate pleasure is suspect, if not downright evil. Of course, we should not assume that John would approve—or disapprove—any or all of these activities, but they do not on the face of it constitute what he regards as the world or the things of the world.

The antithesis of God and the world (v. 15) is basic to what is appropriately called the Johannine dualism. This antithesis should not, however, be construed in terms of the spiritual

65

versus the material—or carnal. The world is, after all, the creation of God through the word (John 1:10). Probably 1 John stands more sharply opposed to the world than does the Gospel. We have already observed that the belief that God loves the world, as well as having created it, is much more clearly represented in the Gospel than in the Epistle. Nevertheless, for both the Gospel and 1 John the world—as it constitutes itself, preserves and cultivates itself, relies upon itself—is enmity to God. To put matters as our text does is probably the best way to describe John's view of the world. He warns the reader against loving the world.

The world then is described in terms of the lusts or desires that it evokes and that reign in it: the lust of the flesh, the lust of the eyes, and the pride of life. Translating this as "sex, money, and power" may not miss the mark by much (NRSV: "the desire of the flesh, the desire of the eyes, the pride in riches"). Still, it would be wrong to see here a simple combination of those things as such. Rather, it is a matter of what a person wills and desires, what one wants and trusts. The placing of things—whether material, mental, or spiritual—in the position of the ultimate object of desire is condemned. John comes rather close here to Paul's indictment of sinful humanity in Romans: "They exchanged the truth about God for a lie and worshiped and served the creature rather than the Creator" (1:25). Finally, the transitoriness of the world and its goods is underscored (v. 17). This transitoriness contrasts with the permanence of God's gift of salvation through Christ. Perhaps surprisingly, the transitoriness of the world is contrasted not with God but with the believer, with the one who does the will of God. John subtly shifts from a description of the world, and the attitudes that govern the world, to the destiny of the one who believes and obeys God, at the same time suggesting the dire fate of the person who puts faith in, and obeys, the world.

We have dealt with the basis and authority of teaching in the early church generally in our discussion of 2:12–14. The specific Johannine teaching about worldliness is plain, as we have just seen. Fearfulness about inculcating a false piety should not, however, deflect the Christian teacher from this text, which is quite basic if rightly understood. The fundamental question raised has to do not with what specific things the Christian should abstain from or condemn, but with the direction of desire and thus of the will. A will rightly oriented desires to believe and obey God and abjures the temptation to pursue anything, even any good, that stands between self and God. This is a simple truth, quite indispensable to a proper understanding and appropriation of the gospel.

What can be taught about this passage is also what should be preached. The fact that 1 John 2:15–17 has been used to support a rather narrow and repressive piety is all the more reason to expound it correctly in the setting of the church. Its message, rightly understood, is quite central to Christian faith—not at all peripheral. Here is a case, like not a few in the Bible, in which a text needs to be rescued from too narrow an interpretation.

REFLECTION:
The Johannine Letters as Pastoral Epistles

The presumption of the brief section (2:12–14) would seem to be the existence of at least two, and perhaps three, Christian generations; we are thus reminded of the Pauline Pastorals, and particularly 2 Timothy 1:5, where Timothy's grandmother Lois and his mother Eunice are mentioned as having been Christian before Timothy. In other respects also there are similarities or analogies with the Pauline Pastorals, so much so that we may with good reason speak of the Johannine Epistles as pastoral letters.

In both cases, problems of right conduct are in view. Are Christians conducting themselves properly? In the Pauline Pastorals we encounter a much greater degree of specificity in the identification of distinct groups of people or church offices. In particular, detailed directions are given for the conduct of women, slaves, bishops, deacons, the wealthy, and so on, so that we get a rather detailed picture of the kinds of people who made up the churches, as well as their organization.

In both cases also there is a clear concern for right teaching (doctrine) that has been brought on by the appearance of false teachers and false teaching within the churches. The problems of the Pauline letters seem more diffuse or diverse in nature, but there may be points of contact with the Johannine. As we

67

shall see, the apparently docetic Christology of the opponents of 1 John (4:1–3) suggests that the author may have had to deal with an incipient or proto-Gnosticism, while 1 Timothy inveighs against "what is falsely called knowledge" (6:20-21)—the Greek word is *gnōsis.* Whether the Pauline Pastorals have the Gnostic heresy in view is a disputed question. They do not seem to combat a docetic Christology, but 1 Timothy 4:1–5 denounces the kind of asceticism common in some later Gnostic groups.

Both sets of issues, moral and doctrinal, raise in a quite practical way the question of the source and seat of authority in the church. By what right does one tell other Christians what is permissible or impermissible by way of teaching or conduct? Again in this case the Pauline Pastorals seem more helpfully specific, if perhaps less profound. As clearly as any New Testament books, these letters attest to the existence of a kind of creedal consensus, and perhaps the beginning of the formation of actual creeds (cf. 1 Tim. 1:15; 2:5–6; 4:9–10; 2 Tim. 1:13–14). Orthodoxy, right teaching, is establishing itself. To enforce such teaching in the church, what we now know as the ordained ministry has emerged (1 Tim. 4:14). Thus we read of bishops, elders, and deacons in these letters; for the first time the three historic levels of ordination are attested together. What is more, it is clear that these ordained men, particularly bishops— women are now restricted to subordinate roles—are charged with responsibility for preserving the purity of church doctrine (Tit. 1:9). In other ways bishops, along with elders and deacons, preside over the administration of the church (cf. 1 Tim. 3:1–7).

Therefore, in what is commonly called polity or church order, there seems to be an obvious difference between the Paulines and the Johannines. There is in the Johannine letters little to suggest the establishment of an ordained, much less hierarchical, ministry. Sometimes the rudimentary forms that we see in the Pauline Pastorals are presumed, and John is interpreted in light of them. But how the slim evidence John provides is to be construed is highly problematic. For example, it is possible to imagine that John, the Elder, is attempting to assert episcopal authority over a church or churches, and that Diotrephes, "who likes to put himself first" (3 John 9–10), is resisting him. But it is also conceivable that Diotrephes's putting himself first means that he is attempting to assume the title or role of bishop. The authorities that John can appeal to are "what was from the beginning" (i.e., Jesus and the tradition stemming from him) and the confession of Jesus as Son of God, which the author at least believes entails believing that Jesus really came in the flesh.

Quite likely the Spirit also functions as an authority in the Johannine community (cf. John 14:26; 16:13), but appeal to the Spirit has now proved a precarious basis for authoritative teaching. One must test the spirits by the criterion of right teaching. Otherwise false teaching may be smuggled in under the guise of spiritual authority (1 John 4:1–3; cf. 1 Cor. 12:1–3). Obviously, the author regards himself as one qualified to administer the confessional test. But by what authority? Paul has appointed Timothy, and elders of the church have laid hands upon him, but who appointed John? His authority would seem to be apostolic, like Paul's. That is, it was given directly by God and by or through the Lord Jesus Christ. While Paul attributes his authority to the risen Christ, John seems to trace his to the witness of the historical, earthly Jesus. Of course, this Jesus is viewed from the standpoint of his present, exalted state. Unlike the Pastorals, the Johannine letters contain no nascent doctrine of apostolic succession, except insofar as the Spirit may provide a living link between then and now. Even the Spirit, however, cannot be a substitute for those who have heard, seen, and touched. If the author of 1 John was not himself such a witness— and there are good reasons for doubting that he was—he is obviously convinced that he stands in closest fellowship *(koinōnia)* with such witnesses.

Yet the modes of authority already being set in place in the Pauline Pastorals would provide the structure for the emerging, catholic church. Here we see not only the beginnings of creedal formation, as well as an ordained ministry and church polity, but also appeal to scripture (2 Tim. 3:16). Whether the scripture spoken of included distinctively Christian books—the beginning of the New Testament—is questionable; probably the author meant the Old Testament, to which Christians had appealed for decades. Nevertheless, the singling out of scripture as a basis of authority, alongside creed and clergy, is significant. The foundation of a kind of authoritative triad has been laid. Of course, one continues to appeal to Jesus himself, who was crucified and will come again (1 Tim. 6:13–16), but his authority is

69

for the present mediated through scripture, creedal confession, and ordained clergy. Prophetic or spiritual inspiration is not denied but is kept under ecclesiastical control (1 Tim. 4:14).

Thus, in the dominant, catholic tradition, the Pauline Pastorals represent the wave of the future. Yet the kind of spontaneous, Spirit-inspired authority characteristic of the Johannine literature did not die out. Its continued existence and viability rest upon the conviction that the authority of God in the gospel can never be limited to structures of church and ministry that are human, and frequently all too human.

Of fundamental importance for the perception of the pastoral character of the Johannine letters is the brief article of Hans Conzelmann, "Was von Anfang war," in the 1954 Bultmann *Festschrift*. He made the case that whereas for the Gospel of John the *archē* ("beginning") was the primordial beginning, in 1 John 1:1 "that which was from the beginning" refers rather to the beginning of the Christian tradition, which has an authoritative and normative role. The importance of Spirit and Spirit inspiration in the Gospel of John is emphasized by Ernst Käsemann in his monograph *The Testament of Jesus*. Käsemann had earlier identified the Johannine author with the Elder of the letters and had argued that he had fallen out of favor with the nascent ecclesiastical orthodoxy, represented by the Diotrephes mentioned in 3 John 9 ("Ketzer und Zeuge," 1951). John continues to appeal to the Spirit, but the problematic character of that appeal becomes evident (cf. 1 John 4:1–6). It is clear that the real, historic beginning *(archē)*, ultimately Jesus, has an indispensable authority for John. How does one assure knowledge of that beginning in such a way as to maintain its normative character? The developing concept of apostolic succession addresses this problem directly. Meanwhile, John struggles with a tension implied by the past *archē* and the authority of the Spirit in the present. The Spirit evokes the *archē*, but what if different prophetic voices claiming Spirit inspiration evoke it in different forms or to different ends?

1 John 2:18–29
The Coming of the Antichrist:
Certainty in the Face of False Teaching

The theme of hostility and opposition, whether divine or human, dominates this section. Although modern editions of the Greek New Testament, the RSV, and other English versions do not agree on paragraphing, there is nevertheless a kind of unity and integrity in the remainder of this chapter. The RSV indicates this by placing a major break between chapters 2 and 3, and we accept that division in treating 2:18–29 as a pericope. Also the Common Lectionary takes 3:1–7 as a lesson, and thus supports the division between 2:29 and 3:1. (The NRSV, however, places the division between vv. 28 and 29.) Nevertheless, themes of 2:28–29 spill over into chapter 3. Most noticeable is the theme of the coming of Jesus (or God) in 2:28, which quickly reappears in 3:2.

Perhaps the most significant thread holding this passage together is eschatology; the present age is moving to a culmination as God and his adversaries intervene in human life. We have already seen this motif (e.g., 2:8), but it now provides structure and unity for the whole. John begins by speaking of the coming of the Antichrist and concludes by reminding his readers of the appearance of Christ himself, which is apparently anticipated in the not-too-distant future. Between the two, the major theme and purpose of reassuring the readers about their status and salvation appears in different ways.

By "children" (2:18) John means the whole community or audience whom he addresses. He warns them of the appearance of the Antichrist, which signals the last hour. The fact that they have heard of the coming of the Antichrist appears to mean that he is some expected apocalyptic figure. Although "Antichrist" is found only in the Johannine letters, the expectation of the appearance of some personification of evil or opposition to God in the last days is fairly common in early Christianity (2 Thess. 2:3–4; Rev. 20:7–8; cf. Mark 13:22).

What is unexpected is the assertion that more than one,

71

indeed many antichrists, have already come. They are not supernatural, apocalyptic figures but apparently John's opponents, schismatic Christians who have left the fellowhip of the community (v. 19). Yet perhaps as modern readers we too easily pose the alternative of either apocalyptic figures or opponents, for the opposition as John conceives it has supernatural overtones. In any event, it is quite clear that John is referring to people, would-be Christians, who have broken with his community and have thereby demonstrated that they never really belonged in the first place (cf. 1 Cor. 11:19). The NRSV translates idiomatically, but accurately, "They did not belong to us." Their defection is in this respect a good thing, for it reveals their true colors. It is also an aspect of John's dualistic mode of thought; those who really belong to Jesus have always belonged to him (cf. John 6:37, 39). In 1 John 4:3 and 2 John 7 these antichrists appear again, and there they are said to deny Jesus' coming in the flesh. The fact that such persons are "deceivers" (2 John 7) confirms their identity with the antichrists spoken of here, for later on John will refer to them as "those who would deceive you" (v. 26). Apparently these deceiving antichrists have somehow called into question the adequacy of the readers' faith, as well as their loyalty to John and his teaching.

Against the challenge represented by the false teaching of the antichrist-schismatics, John reassures his readers of their anointing by the Holy One and of their adequate knowledge (v. 20). Although in the Gospel Jesus himself is once called the Holy One of God, and in Revelation "Holy One" twice refers to Jesus (3:7; 16:5), here the work of the Holy Spirit is almost certainly in view as well. Of course, in the Gospel of John the Spirit does nothing other than the work of Christ himself (cf. John 14:16). Whether the anointing spoken of in verses 20 and 26 refers to baptism or to a sealing with oil after baptism that later became a part of the baptismal ritual can no longer be determined. Yet that there is a reference to the initial and continuing work of the Holy Spirit upon the believer is clear enough. Moreover, the knowledge thereby imparted and received is perfectly adequate and sufficient (vv. 20, 27). Yet the fact that John needs to reassure his readers of their knowledge, to remind them that they know the truth, strongly implies that the adequacy of their knowledge has been challenged, presumably by the antichrist-schismatics.

In typical dualistic fashion, one pole of the dyad suggests its opposite. Thus to speak of truth evokes the lie (vv. 21–22), and immediately the liar is identified: the one who denies that Jesus is the Christ. Obviously the antithesis of this denial is the true confession that Jesus is the Christ. Conceivably, the opposition has already accused John, or his party in the disputes, of lying or not imparting to the community the whole or a higher truth. If so, what we have here would be a kind of parry and counterthrust. But this remains speculation. John's dualistic way of thinking and the presence of opposition would suffice to account for his language. More important, and fortunately more discernible, is the nature of the false teaching John opposes. Obviously, the dispute concerns the claim that Jesus is the Christ, the Son of God.

What has been denied, and why is John so urgent in his determination to set matters straight? Taken out of context, the statements of verses 22–23 could have in view non-Christians who deny that Jesus is the Christ or the Son of God. One thinks immediately of the Jewish opposition to Jesus, those who reject his claims in the Gospel of John. Yet such opposition is not mentioned in 1 John, while in the entire letter and in the immediate context of this pericope the opposition spoken of, or alluded to, is clearly intra-Christian opposition. These are people who have split off from John's church. We are witness to a dispute among Christians over church doctrine. If this is the case, the opponents' denial that Jesus is the Christ and their denial of the Son can hardly be taken at face value. That is, it can hardly be the case that they simply reject the Christian claim and confession altogether.

Inasmuch as the Antichrist and the question of the right confession of Jesus Christ appear also in 4:1–3 and 2 John 7, it is reasonable to look there for the key to understand this passage. When we do, we find that what is at issue is the fleshliness, the humanity, of Jesus, which the opponents deny or do not confess. Thus they presumably deny that *Jesus* was the Christ (not that Jesus was the *Christ*), and their denial of the Son is therefore a denial that Jesus, this man, this entirely human individual, was the Son. What they deny is, not that there was a Christ or that there was a Son, but that the man Jesus was truly that Christ and Son of God. With the change of fronts from Jewish (in the Gospel) to intra-Christian (in 1 John), the points of denial or controversy have seemingly reversed themselves. In the Gospel, over against the presumption that Jesus was a

73

man but nothing more or other than a human being, it was necessary to insist that this man was the Christ, the Son of God (cf. 20:30–31). In the Epistle, over against the (heretical Christian) presumption that the Christ, the Son of God, had been revealed in human appearance only, but had not come to live and die in the flesh, it was necessary to insist that he was the truly human Jesus. The ancient Christian heresy that denied the humanity of Jesus was called Docetism (from the Greek *dokein*, "to seem") because it held that Jesus only seemed to be human. We apparently have an early form of that heresy here in 1 John, although exactly what these opponents believed is impossible to reconstruct on the basis of the Johannine letters.

What the believers have heard from the beginning (v. 24) is the word of Jesus, the word about Jesus—thus in some sense Jesus himself. From the standpoint of 1 John, Jesus is available only through the word of witness (1:1–4). But the language of abiding is elsewhere used of Jesus himself and the believer (John 15:1–11; cf. 14:23; increasingly in 1 John chaps. 3 and 4). In what seems to be an intentional reference to the letter's prologue, where Jesus is called "the word of life" (1:1), the note of promise is now struck (v. 25). What in the present abides in the believer has its fruition in eternal life. Such a reference to "the beginning" as we find in 2:24 is clearly an allusion to Jesus himself; at the same time it emphasizes the role and antiquity of the tradition that originates with Jesus. What is heard from the beginning is the ancient and authentic word of tradition— the word of and about Jesus—that stands in stark contrast to the recent words of the separatists, the deceivers.

Not surprisingly, the deceivers are referred to once more (v. 26). That they are purveyors of a false teaching is implied by the following statement (v. 27) about the believers' original anointing. The anointing that the readers have received from Jesus ("from him") probably consisted of both baptism and its accompanying, or preceding, catechetical instruction. That anointing in deed and word is trustworthy and true, "no lie." Quite likely, the solemn asseveration that it is "no lie" reflects the charges of the opponents. Stick with what you have been taught from the beginning, John is saying. Do not let the false teachers lead you astray or undercut your security and confidence by questioning your anointing. What you have been taught is no lie; rather, they are liars! Possibly the anointing and teaching

74

will assist the true believers in identifying true and false spirits (4:1–3).

As John returns to the matter of the opponents, the antichrists and deceivers, so now he again strikes the eschatological note with which he had begun this section. Here it no longer has an ominous ring and yet there remains more than a hint of warning (v. 28). Plainly, those who abide in Christ, which means abiding in his baptism and the original teaching about him, will have confidence and no cause for shame at his coming. The nuance of warning overlaps a foundation of assurance. Basic knowledge of the righteousness of Christ, which belongs to all believers, reassures all who do the right thing that they are, in fact, born of him (v. 29). Do not let anybody tell you anything different, says John, or require of you any more! This final word of reassurance, in the face of those who would unsettle his readers, ties verse 29 to what precedes and justifies the division between 2:29 and 3:1.

If one asks what Christian teaching is found in this pericope or what the Christian teacher is to make of it, the answer is not altogether obvious. Much of its content is closely related to the setting and situation of the letter, the controversy with the opponents to which it is addressed (vv. 18–19, 26). The polemic is sharp indeed. The most significant christological issue touched upon (vv. 22–23) is not dealt with in such a way that the point is immediately obvious. It comes out only in comparison with other passages (4:1–8; 2 John 7). The anointing that is spoken of several times and seems to figure largely in the discussion (vv. 20, 27) is not defined or described directly; we can only infer what is meant. The Antichrist is apparently an apocalyptic figure whose advent was expected in anticipation of the epiphany of Christ and the final judgment (v. 28). Christ's epiphany is mentioned, not in a threatening manner, but with the assurance that all will be well if the believers abide in him (v. 28; cf. vv. 24, 27). The underlying purpose and leading motif of this section is the reassurance of the community of believers, particularly in view of the attempt of the "deceivers" or "antichrists" to lure the faithful after them. Apparently they have begun by trying to persuade John's followers that what they have heard and received from the beginning is somehow wrong or inadequate and that Christians should follow them instead. Against

75

them John assures the readers of the sufficiency of what they already have and encourages them to abide in Jesus (vv. 27–28) or in what they have heard from the beginning, telling them that he is writing not because they do not know the truth but because they do. The important motif of reassurance in this passage will probably be of greater use for preaching than for teaching. The various elements of Christian teaching that appear here are more adequately presented elsewhere in the letter.

Although this pericope is not included in the Common Lectionary, it offers an opportunity for the preacher precisely because of the way in which John seeks to reassure his audience. The analogies between the situation John faced and the late twentieth-century religious situation are significant. The references to antichrists, liars, and deceivers, however, open the door to preachers who want to see in these shadowy figures of the past references to the people or parties in the church whom they themselves wish to defame or discredit. This is usually not a practice that reflects much credit upon the preacher.

On the other hand, the text offers a firm basis for the preacher to reassure his congregation of the adequacy of the teaching and baptism that they have already received. Such reassurance, set against the backdrop of efforts to undercut their confidence, is far from irrelevant today. The opponents of 1 John were not the last to unsettle other Christians by claiming or implying that their access to the truth, to the Spirit, to God, or to Christ was flawed or blocked by their lack of knowledge or spiritual attainment or experience. In some kinds of rather negative Christian preaching, such tactics have often been used to play on people's uncertainties or have been framed in such a way as to create them. Such felt uncertainty then leaves people vulnerable to the claims of those who offer a better or more certain way. Against precisely such tactics John strikes back, insisting that the original and true confession of Jesus Christ and obedience to him are grounds fully sufficient for the believer's assurance before God: "If you know that he is righteous, you may be sure that every one who does right is born of him" (2:29). John offers the kind of reassurance that cuts through religious or quasispiritual pretensions designed to intimidate people and gets back to basics.

1 John 3:1–3
The Father's Love: Children of God Now

The related themes of the love of God and being children of God are taken up and expanded upon in 3:1–3. Although the readers have already been addressed as children, now for the first time John considers what it may mean to be children of God. Love within the fellowship and love for God have already been the focus of attention. Now, however, John speaks of the meaning of God's love for us. Although many commentators have taken 2:28–29 with 3:1–3, and sometimes with following verses, as a single section, we have already observed that the RSV's division between 2:29 and 3:1 makes sense. (Probably the NRSV's taking 2:29 with 3:1–3 is based on the common theme of being born of God, or of Christ, and, therefore, being children of God.) Obviously, the theme of Christ's coming holds chapters 2 and 3 together (especially 2:28 and 3:2).

The consequence and proof of the love of God is being, and being called, children of God. The love of God is described as a gift, which means that we do nothing to merit it. This description of God's love accords exactly with what we read later on in 1 John about the priority of God's love (4:8–10). While the prior love of God may be the unspoken ground of the saving work of Christ already described (e.g., 1:7; 2:1), only now does the reader encounter an explicit statement of this fact.

As soon as this love and acceptance are affirmed, however, their opposite comes into view. The world's failure to acknowledge believers as children of God is grounded in its ignorance of God himself. Thus the theme of the world (cf. 2:15–17) is taken up again, and after the denunciation of the opponents or antichrists (2:18–27), it is clear enough that they also continue in view. They are the primary representatives of the world (cf. 4:5) as it encroaches upon the Johannine community.

No sooner is the world mentioned, however, than it is left behind as John returns to the theme of the appearance of Christ (vv. 2–3). In fact, verse 2 could be taken to refer to the appearance of God, for "God" is the nearest possible antecedent of the pronoun "him." Yet since Jesus seems to be the one who ap-

77

pears, or comes, in 2:28, and because the one who appeared to take away sins (3:5) is clearly Jesus, it makes sense to see here a reference to Jesus as well. Also, "he" in 3:3, "he is pure" (RSV), translates the Greek *ekeinos,* "that one," which in 1 John is characteristically used of Jesus. Moreover, the promise that we shall be like him takes up the admonition to walk as Jesus walked (2:6).

The uncertainty implied by our not knowing what we shall be (v. 2) is more than offset by the assurance that we are already ("now") God's children. It is an entirely safe assumption that we shall be something better rather than worse. In other words, the uncertainty leaves the believer in a state of hopeful expectation: "We shall see him as he is." Have Christians not yet seen Jesus as he really is? The disciples at least saw the earthly Jesus, but even they were not able to see him as he was (or is). After his death, their postresurrection knowledge of him perfected the inadequacy of their earlier seeing. Most believers have not seen Jesus at all (John 20:29). The promise to "see him as he is" is a relevant and hopeful one, especially when accompanied by the reassurance that "we shall be like him." It is, in fact, a reiteration of the prayer and promise of Jesus that his disciples should be with him in heaven to behold the glory that he had before creation (John 17:24).

The final note (v. 3) sounds a bit strange because the idea of purification, especially ritual purification, is quite foreign to modern, secular people. It is, of course, an idea common to most ancient religions and particularly prominent in Judaism. There and elsewhere it had already received an ethical interpretation, and so it does in 1 John (cf. vv. 4–10). Basically, the process of purification rids people and their immediate environment of pollution. In ancient Judaism and early Christianity this pollution was already understood largely (if not exclusively) in ethical terms as the pollution of sin, but the religious and social basis of the concept is much broader. The Apostle Paul, for example, shrinks back in horror from the pollution or impurity inherent in a man's living with his father's wife (1 Cor. 5:9–13; cf. the general concept of impurity already expressed in vv. 6–8; also 2 Cor. 6:14—7:1). Impurity is not only sinful, it is ominously shocking. Perhaps in modern American society the concept of obscenity preserves, if in wraithlike form, an element of the sense of impurity that was once well-nigh universal.

The teaching of God's love for us is characteristic of the Johannine literature; it is a major theme of the Gospel of John (3:16). Although for good reason Christians would likely think that Jesus taught God's love for humanity in the other Gospels also, this is not quite the case. God's love is a reasonable inference from his fatherly care, as exemplified in the Parable of the Prodigal Son (Luke 15:11–32) or such sayings as those about anxiety in the Sermon on the Mount (Matt. 6:25–33; cf. Luke 12:22–31). The Lord's Prayer seems to presuppose God's loving care (Matt. 6:9–13) as well. There is, of course, also the biblical, Old Testament theme of God's love and care for Israel expressed so poignantly in the Book of Hosea (11:1–4). Moreover, God's love would seem to undergird statements of Jesus about the character of his own ministry (e.g., Mark 10:45). Nevertheless, while Jesus calls upon people to love their neighbors and enemies, as well as God himself (Mark 12:29–30), he does not explicitly teach the love of God for humanity. That such love is a legitimate inference from his teaching and ministry, however, would seem clear, not only from the synoptic tradition, but also from several crucial statements of the Apostle Paul (e.g., Rom. 5:8; 8:38–39), although Paul, like Jesus, more often speaks of the love that disciples or believers should show to one another.

Although the love of God for humanity is not mentioned as frequently in the New Testament as we might think, the prominence of the theme of God's love in the Gospel and Epistles of John comes as no great surprise to the reader, for it seems to sum up the gospel message of the New Testament. Yet, as we have earlier observed in the case of the love commandment, John's focus is primarily upon the community or church. The Gospel clearly states God's love for the world (3:16). Although 1 John comes close to, but seems to avoid, saying that God loved the world, in the context of speaking of God's love, the author calls Jesus the Savior of the world (4:14). Still, the community of believers, the church, is the arena in which God's love is received and accepted. Therefore, it is only from within the church, and for the church, that the author can speak in a valid way of God's love. The statement that God is love (4:8, 16) is not an abstract, philosophical thesis but an inference from the experience of God's grace in Jesus Christ. God's gift of love is inextricably bound up with the gift of God's Son in life and death. Only the children of God can speak authentically of God's love, even

79

as in human relationships only those who love and are loved can speak of love as an experienced reality rather than as an abstraction or an unfulfilled yearning.

The status of being children of God is then a gift or the effect of the gift of God's love. Therefore, no one should boast that she or he is a child of God, for then the new status is viewed as an accomplishment or work rather than a gift. The Johannine conviction of God's priority and God's election (4:10), shared by Paul (Rom. 8:31–39), is the logical correlative of the assurance of God's love and grace. The doctrine of God's election speaks to the question of how I, a sinner, come to stand within God's grace rather than to the question of whether or not I have free will. I experience free will, but that freedom only becomes a possibility within the realm of God's grace when I am no longer enslaved to sin.

The eschatological teaching of this passage is stated unmistakably but subtly (v. 2). It is characteristic of Christian eschatology to speak with reserve or in a veiled way about the eschatological future, that is, life beyond death or in the kingdom of God. The most famous example is Paul's statement in 1 Corinthians 13:12: "For now we see in a mirror dimly, but then face to face. Now I know in part; then I shall understand fully, even as I have been fully understood." John's affirmation here is of a piece with Paul's, marked by confidence but also by modesty and reserve. Unfortunately, Christians have sometimes been misled by taking the Book of Revelation to be a series of predictions about future worldly events rather than apocalyptic imagery or symbolism and consequently have abandoned this necessary and appropriate modesty and reserve. For our time and our knowledge, the most important fact about the eschatological future is its Christocentricity. That is, what we shall be will be modeled after who Christ is, and even that can only be fully known when the time comes.

The final, indirect admonition about purification is explicitly related to this future hope. Verse 3 reads literally, "everyone who has this hope in him purifies himself, as that one is pure." The demonstrative pronoun "that one" (Greek *ekeinos*) refers to Jesus, as is usually the case when it is used in 1 John. Christian life in this world can be viewed as a response to God's love, as obedience to Christ's commands, or as purification (i.e., preparation) in hope. Although not put in exactly those terms, we have here a kind of test case of those who truly hope in

Christ: they purify themselves as Jesus Christ is pure. That is, they live in response to God's love and in obedience to Christ's commands.

The Common Lectionary limits the epistle reading for All Saints' Day in the A cycle to 1 John 3:1–3. Interestingly enough, the Gospel lesson is Matthew 5:1–12, the Beatitudes of the Sermon on the Mount. While God's love is not mentioned explicitly in the Beatitudes, the blessings Jesus offers obviously stem from God and are expressions of God's loving care and concern for the poor, the meek, the hungry, the merciful, and the like. The miracle of God's love is no less plainly articulated here.

The lesson for the third Sunday of Easter (cycle B) is 1 John 3:1–7. Apparently continuity between verses 1–3 and 4–7 is seen in the fact that the notion of purification, with its Jewish sacrificial background, suggests the possibility of sin, which is then dealt with in verses 4–7(11). John's thought is continuous and interlocking, so that this continuity cannot be denied. But the Common Lectionary, by stopping with verse 7, conveniently omits the really difficult and awkward parts of this section. Thus the preacher who selects this lesson as the text for preaching is presumably spared having to comment on "he who commits sin is of the devil" (v. 8) or to explain the assertion that the one born of God *cannot* sin (v. 9).

For the purpose of preaching, the shorter reading for All Saints' Day is preferable. The preacher who cannot find enough to say about 3:1–3 will scarcely take comfort in what follows. Furthermore, as in verses 1–3, there is an obvious integrity of theme or subject matter in verses 4–10, the succeeding RSV paragraph. We find there John's discussion of the nature and origin of sin, difficult as it may be for the ears of most Christians. This discussion is then elaborated in relation to love and the love commandment in 3:11–18.

Perhaps the intention of the Lectionary is to encourage the preacher to develop the themes of sin and righteousness after John's statement about the believers' status as children of God in verses 1–3. Thus the imperative is set alongside the indicative, and Christians are not allowed to rest on their laurels, so to speak. If so, well and good. On the other hand, it is arguable that much of so-called mainline, particularly American, Christianity suffers from an inadequate sense of the indicative, what God has done. Christianity has for so long been interpreted as

81

an ethical standard, an inspiration to action, or as providing a social or political agenda, that its essential, declarative element is often lost. It is important to recognize that 1 John begins with a message, God is light (1:5), and only then unfolds in ethical terms what being or walking in that light must mean. Nevertheless, the walking in the light is not itself the light. The light has a priority, a givenness, apart from which there would be no point in talking about walking in it. While it is incontestably true that the light becomes darkness for those unwilling to walk in it, this does not negate the prior reality and independent existence of the light. The light can be light for walking only if it is really and truly light. What is said of light could, of course, equally well be said of love. God's light is his love. John does not make that equation, but it is an obvious and true one. A sermon on 1 John 3:1–3 would naturally emphasize the givenness and priority of God's love and of the status of individual believers, as well as of the community, as children of God. This is a message sufficient for preaching and worth hearing.

1 John 3:4–10
Sin Is Lawlessness: Can It Be Avoided?

John does not develop a doctrine or theory of sin as alienation from God in the way Paul does (cf. Rom. 1:18—3:20). Nevertheless, what John has to say about sin here fits the Pauline doctrine rather well. Sin is a condition—John describes it as lawlessness (v. 4)—from which humanity needs to be freed by the work of Christ. Once freed from sin, the believer should—indeed, must—live for God and remain free from sin. This point, which John states rather clearly, is made also by the Apostle Paul, if in somewhat different terms (Rom. 6:15–23).

What John means by "lawlessness" (*anomia*, a state of being without law) is a good question. "Lawlessness" could imply that salvation consists in the restoration of what has been lost, namely, the law, but that does not seem to be what John means, for nowhere else in 1 John is the Old Testament law mentioned. When in the Gospel John speaks of the law or portrays Jesus speaking of it, there is a certain ambivalence: The law is valid, but effecting obedience to law is not what the mission and

82

message of Jesus are about. The suggestion that by "lawlessness" John is referring to an evil or iniquity that will prevail in the end time (cf. the use of *anomia* in Matt. 24:11–12; 7:22–23; 2 Cor. 6:14–15; 2 Thess. 2:3) is attractive in view of his description of the opponents in apocalyptic terms. Lawlessness characterizes an era in which antichrists appear.

The statement that Jesus appeared to take away sin (v. 5) agrees with what has been said earlier on (1:7; 2:1), and the assertion that "in him there is no sin" seems a logical inference. (As we have already noticed, the NRSV consistently translates *phaneroun* "reveal," or, as here, the aorist passive "was revealed," rather than "appear"; the terms are closely related, but have somewhat different connotations, in that "reveal" implies the manifestation of something or someone previously hidden.) John sets up an antinomy between sin and Jesus; it is not too much to say between sin as lawlessness or the final, eschatological iniquity and Jesus as righteousness or the final, eschatological salvation. One has to abide in one realm or the other. This way of understanding life reflects the Johannine dualism, which we have been encountering at every turn. Thus when we read that for the one who abides in Jesus sin is excluded (v. 6), and that the person who sins (Greek: "is sinning") has neither seen nor known him, we should not be surprised.

The further statements then seem almost truisms (vv. 7–8). The allusion to deceivers, however, should not be missed. The antichrists (2:18), separatists (2:19), and deceivers (2:26) who have previously been mentioned are likely still in view in verse 7. That is, the possibility of the readers being deceived is not an abstract, hypothetical possibility. Rather it represents a distinct threat from a specific quarter that the author knows all too well. "Don't let them confuse you," John is saying. Things are ultimately quite simple. It all boils down to a choice of one way or the other; either to be righteous as Christ (Greek: *ekeinos*, "that one") is righteous or to sin and to choose the lot of the devil, "who has sinned from the beginning." Thus the one who sins can said to be "of the devil" (RSV, v. 8) or even "a child of the devil" (NRSV, exercising some interpretative license, presumably in light of John 8:44: "You are of your father the devil"). Here the familiar Johannine "from the beginning" occurs in a strange context and refers, of course, not to the beginning of the Christian tradition but to the primordial beginning (cf. John

1:1). The devil has always been evil (cf. John 8:44). To choose sin is to side with the devil whose works Jesus came to destroy. That is unthinkable, and so we are prepared for John's next, rather startling statement.

In verse 9 John declares and reiterates that everyone who is born of God does not sin. (This is the form the Greek statement takes; that is, the subject is positive and the verb is negated, but it amounts to the same thing as the RSV. The NRSV translation negates the verb, as the Greek does.) Moreover, he or she is said to be unable to sin because God's seed (so NRSV; RSV, "nature") abides in him or her. The imagery of rebirth, or better, birth from above (i.e., from God) is found in Jesus' conversation with Nicodemus (John 3). In saying that God's seed abides in the Christian, 1 John continues the graphic reproductive imagery of the Gospel. In the Gospel, however, there is no explicit discussion of whether one who is so born is prevented from sinning. Nicodemus does not even understand what Jesus is saying. In 1 John 3:9, however, the author writes to those who can claim to be born again, that is, from God.

The problem is, of course, that this statement seems not only to fly in the face of experience but also to contradict what has been said in 1:8, 10; 2:1, where sin by believers seems to be in view. In fact, the claim to have no sin is there presented as reprehensible. Is John caught in a hopeless contradiction? Probably most Christians would agree with 1 John 1:8, 10; 2:1 and would wonder how 3:9 could possibly be true, even if it did not contradict the earlier passages. Commentators have not found a way around this contradiction, and some (e.g., Rudolf Bultmann) have resorted to a source-critical resolution of the problem, that is, to the suggestion that we really have two hands at work in 1 John. One writer is a perfectionist, and the other not only believes that Christians can sin but that it is important that they not deny this fact.

John Wesley, for whom Christian perfection was an overriding concern, preached and published a sermon on this verse in which he conceded at the outset that those born of God have nevertheless sinned:

> It is plain, in fact, that those whom we cannot deny to have been truly born of God (the Spirit of God having given us in his word this infallible testimony concerning them), nevertheless, not only could, but did, commit sin, even gross, outward sin. They did

transgress the plain, known laws of God, speaking or acting what
they knew he had forbidden (Sermon XV.ii.3).

Wesley then goes on to instance from scripture David and
Bathsheba and the Apostle Peter at Antioch. For him John's
statement must mean: "But 'whosoever is born of God,' while
he abideth in faith and love, and in the spirit of prayer and
thanksgiving, not only doth not, but cannot, thus commit sin"
(Sermon XV.ii.2).

Some such interpretation of John's statement has been
adopted by many exegetes. It makes sense with reference not
only to 1 John's earlier statements but to common Christian
experience through the centuries. For Wesley, in the authority
of scripture, and specific instances in which biblical figures who
must be regarded as born of God have sinned, we have a context and standard for interpreting 1 John 3:9 in such a way as
to bring it into line with 1:8, 10, and 2:1. In our effort to understand this statement, we side with Wesley against modern
source critics at least to this extent: We want to interpret intelligibly the text as it stands in the letter.

To this end, the interpretation of the final statement of our
paragraph (v. 10) may shed some light on the problem. The
phrase "by this" with which this sentence begins can refer to
what has just been said, or it can refer to the latter part of the
sentence itself. The RSV (and NRSV), by its use of the colon
before "whoever does not do right is not of God, nor he who
does not love his brother," takes it in this latter way. But "by
this" can as easily refer to what has already been said in verse
9. In this case, the final clause (v. 10b) would afford an appropriate transition to the reiteration and exposition of the love commandment that follows (vv. 11–18). Then in verse 10 we should
have a period marking the break in the middle of the verse
(after ". . . of the devil") rather than a colon. The remainder of
the verse would begin a new paragraph.

What difference would that make for the interpretation of
verse 9? To take verse 10a as the conclusion of the section
beginning at 3:4 makes clear that its subject is the identification
of the children of God and the children of the devil. All along,
the opponents of John—the schismatics, antichrists, or deceivers—have been in view (2:18–19, 26; 3:7). In John's opinion,
they are in league with the devil; here his dualistic perspective

85

comes into play. What they have been saying to the community is never stated as specifically as we would like, but John's description of them as deceivers and his effort to rally the community around the right confession and the love commandment while at the same time offering reassurance is suggestive. Are they in John's eyes not only deviant in doctrine but committing "gross, outward sin" while claiming that they cannot sin? Quite probably. If so, then John's statements of verses 4–8 would relate to them, in the sense that the entire discussion has their claims in view. He would, however, expect his readers to recognize their sin for what it is. Quite possibly John also has these opponents in mind when he discusses the transgression of Jesus' love commandment in 3:11–18. In verse 9 he would, so to speak, throw their claims to perfection back into their face. Their gross, outward sin exposes them for who they truly are, showing them to be children of the devil rather than of God.

Not that John himself is not serious about what he writes in verse 9 as far as Christians are concerned. Christ's saving death effects cleansing (and freedom) from sin, and he writes the community with some urgency to prevent them from sinning (2:1). This work of Christ brings about the birth from God that is freedom from sin, but a freedom that must be ratified by continually willing and doing what is right, as John never tires of urging. In his opponents he sees a moral lassitude and flagrant sinfulness accompanied by claims of invulnerability guaranteed by birth from God. Thus he can characterize them for who they are (v. 8) and perhaps quote their own motto against them (v. 9) to show that their claims not only to perfection, but especially to birth from God, are wholly specious. If the definition of sin as "eschatological iniquity" be accepted, the sinfulness of the opponents would fit with their designation as antichrists. They are the manifestation and personification of the evil that is to appear before the return of Jesus.

Such a scenario as we have briefly sketched is admittedly hypothetical. Nevertheless, it draws upon hints and bits of evidence that we find in the text. It is avowedly an effort to rescue 1 John from self-contradiction, but such an effort is justifiable because the self-contradiction seems so blatant. The author, or even an editor, could not help but notice it. The presumption that whoever is responsible for this text could not have missed the seeming contradiction thus leads us to seek a context, in this case an historical context, in which it becomes intelligible.

What teaching is then to be sought in this pericope? Obviously, if our understanding is correct, it should not be used in support of a kind of born-again perfectionism. We have interpreted it against a putative historical background, which the letter at best only partially reveals. Wesley interpreted the statement of verse 9 against a biblical background on the basis of his then widely shared understanding of the authority, indeed the infallibility, of scripture. That is, he argued that because to take this statement at its seeming face value is to fly in the face of what scripture elsewhere teaches, it cannot mean that it is really impossible for a person who has been genuinely born again (i.e., from God) ever to commit sin. Of course, what scripture teaches is borne out in our own experience and perception.

Preoccupation with the apparent difficulty of verse 9 should not prevent us from paying attention to the major motif of this pericope, which is the heinousness, and obviousness, of sin. Sin is not here perceived or portrayed as something hidden or subtle; it is open and blatant. It may well be that conscientious Christians too often bemuse themselves, or lose their perspective, in contemplating the possibilities and pitfalls of subtle forms of sin in their own lives, while ignoring blatant sinfulness in the form of outrageous transgressions all around them. It is often difficult to credit media reports of "gross, outward sin," whether in government, business, or religious circles because we are unable even to conceive of what people will think they can get away with—and presumably often do! John's bracing and forthright depiction and characterization of sin is worth attending to, as is his refusal to allow Christians to get off the hook by compromising with sin in their own lives.

Preaching from this pericope may be difficult, as the Common Lectionary's division already anticipates. By offering the preacher 3:1–7, it leaves off the harsh words about the devil and his children as well as the statement about those born of God being unable to sin, with which we have wrestled. Perhaps the preacher should take a hint from the Lectionary and take a vacation from this text—unless, of course, he agrees with John that the reality and blatancy of sin are a sufficient threat to the well-being and lives of others to be worthy of our attention. Moreover, the strong element of reassurance to believers that pervades this letter is in evidence here. To say that "no one who

87

sins has either seen him or known him" may sound harsh and in need of circumspect qualification. On the other hand, in times when all sorts of malefaction, particularly among those claiming the protective cloak of religion, go unchecked or even unnoticed, such a rejection of pious pretension comes as a breath of fresh air. Those who seem to be getting away with murder are only demonstrating who they really are. In this the obedient believer may find reassurance.

1 John 3:11–18
The Message You Have Heard From the Beginning: The Love Commandment Again

The mention of failure to love one's brother or sister (3:10) recalls Jesus' command to love one another (3:11; cf. John 13:34), which is the message the community and Christians generally have heard from the beginning (cf. 2:7 and our discussion of the old commandment). There is a certain amount of repetition now, but repetition does not faze our author; it is a means of driving the message home. The commandment of mutual love is the basis of community *(koinōnia)*.

As Brown has observed in his commentary, 3:11 marks a turning point in the letter. This is the second mention of the message (Brown: "gospel") the readers have heard from the beginning or from Jesus (1:5). From this point on, as Brown observes, increased emphasis falls upon love within the community rather than hostility from without. Thus the division of the main body of 1 John into two parts, 1:5—3:10 and 3:11—5:12 (or 13), seems justified, both by these nearly identical markers and by the subtle shift in content. The shift parallels a similar, if more pronounced, shift between John chapters 12 and 13, as Jesus' conflict with "the Jews" is displaced by his ministry to his disciples who together with him draw away from the world in preparation for his death. Particularly if 1 John is to be understood as a kind of commentary on the Gospel of John, such a division is apposite and helpful. On the other hand, the intelligibility of what follows in 1 John cannot be said to depend upon it.

88

As an illustration of the necessity of love, we now encounter something new, and only here in 1 John, namely, the reference to an Old Testament figure, Cain (cf. Heb. 11:4; Jude 11). It was Cain, of course, who out of jealousy killed his brother because the Lord preferred Abel's offering to his own (Gen. 4:1–16). According to the Genesis account, Cain was angry and his face fell (4:5). That Cain was of the evil one (i.e., Satan; 1 John 3:12) puts him on the side of the antichrists John opposes. That the murder was the result of Cain's jealousy, as Genesis makes clear, is at least recognizable from John's statement that his own deeds were evil while his brother's were righteous. It is not obvious from Genesis, however, that apart from the offerings Abel's deeds were righteous while Cain's were evil. Perhaps this view of Cain rests on later traditions in which he becomes an archetypal evildoer (Jude 11; cf. Brown, pp. 441–443), although it may be the author's own understanding of the meaning of God's rejecting Cain's offering. One may even reason that John could not have conceived of Abel's offering being accepted and Cain's rejected unless Cain had been an evil person, but this goes beyond our text.

What is clear enough is that Cain's murder of his brother Abel affords an apt instance of the consequence of failing to heed the love commandment. The opposite of love for one's brother is hatred leading to murder (v. 15). John does not quote Cain's famous question, "Am I my brother's keeper?" (Gen. 4:9), but in his view the correct answer would doubtless be "Yes!" The motif of hatred as murder probably harks back to the Gospel (John 8:37–44), where Jesus accuses his adversaries, or their father the devil, of being murderers (especially 8:44). In view of the Johannine dualism, it is not surprising that where love is not shared, there is hatred; no compromise or mediating position is conceivable. Thus it should be no source of astonishment that the world hates the beloved community (v. 13); Jesus had already warned his disciples of that hatred (John 15:18–20). Presumably it is based upon the same kind of jealousy that motivated Cain to kill his brother. Certainly the world's deeds are evil while the Christian community's deeds, done in love, are good. The integral relationship of love to life and hatred to death (v. 14) should by now not surprise us, for hatred is not only death-dealing but belongs to that realm of darkness (2:9) which death and sin also inhabit.

The definition of love, like that of hatred, is given in narra-

89

tive form; John refers to the death of Jesus as a model for love (v. 16), thus echoing Jesus' own words in the Gospel (15:12–13). As those who hate are murderers, following in the wake of Cain, so those who love are life-givers, following Jesus. The narrative of Cain leads to hatred and death; that of Jesus to love and life. Here is a brief but fundamental exercise in narrative theology and ethics.

John follows this theological exercise, cast in his typically dualistic framework, with a down-to-earth and specific example and admonition (3:17–18). Love's genuineness is demonstrated in concrete acts of helpfulness. Obviously, to refuse to perform such acts is to close one's heart. The disposition of one's heart includes a willingness to act, apart from which it is meaningless to speak of love (v. 18). Because verse 18 follows naturally after verse 17, the RSV's paragraph division between verse 18 and verse 19 seems more natural than the NRSV's division between verses 17 and 18. Love in "word or speech" is not really love at all. The Letter of James expresses a similar point of view (1:22; 2:16), as does Jesus in the Sermon on the Mount (Matt. 7:16–20). What is at stake is not accomplishments or results but the demonstration of the existence of genuine love through a willingness to act. John seems to abhor speech, even sound theological speech, that is not undergirded by a corresponding willingness to act in love toward one's fellow believer (cf. 1 John 4:20).

Once again John develops the central Christian teaching on love in his characteristic way (cf. 2:7–11 and commentary). Although now he characterizes the love commandment as "the message" (3:11; cf. 1:5), it is clear what he has in view. Significantly, the "message" of 1:5 is that God is light and in him is no darkness whatever; but, as it turns out, that message is closely related to the love commandment. Walking in the light means loving one's fellow believer (cf. 1:6; 2:9–11). Indeed, the source of all such human love is revealed to be God's love abiding in the believer (v. 17: ". . . how does God's love abide in him?").

At the beginning of this section (v. 11) the Christian teaching on love is rooted in Jesus ("from the beginning"). John, like no other Epistle writer, grounds the authority of his message in the message of Jesus. John embodies and demonstrates the antiquity of the conviction among Christians that what can be traced back to Jesus is most profoundly relevant and true. Here, as in 2:7–11, the contrast between love and hate is sharply drawn, an expression of John's dualistic mode of thought. In fact, the hatred, and perhaps particularly the hatred of the world for the beloved community, is personified and illustrated in Cain, who for the moment serves as a kind of antitype to Christ. The teaching of love is now grounded not only in Jesus' words but also in his action, his death. Again, one calls to mind the word of the Gospel (15:12–13) and is also reminded of what Paul wrote about Christ's death (Rom. 5:8): "God shows his love for us in that while we were yet sinners Christ died for us." Interestingly, in Paul's statement the subject who loves is God, where in the context one would have expected Christ (but cf. Gal. 2:20, where the subject is Christ). Yet the difference is more apparent than real, for what is attributed to Christ by way of saving and loving purpose in John can also be attributed to God (cf. John 3:16).

As we have already observed, John's understanding of what it means to love is quite down-to-earth and practical (3:17–18). Will or intention is closely bound with action. Talk is cheap. Not actually doing something for brothers or sisters in need is to close one's heart against them. Love is not just a special way of feeling; it is an orientation of life and action.

The preaching values of this pericope are obvious enough and do not need to be belabored. The concluding emphasis on the necessity of actually doing something will appeal to preachers and congregations alike and is a point well worth making. The Common Lectionary (and now NRSV) begins a lesson with 3:18 and continues it through 3:24. The theme of love then reappears in verse 23, forming a kind of inclusion with verse 18. It seems obvious, however, that verse 18 is a reiteration, in somewhat more abstract terms, of what has already been said more concretely in verse 17, and therefore to split verse 18 away from verse 17 would be unnatural. On the other hand, the opening address of verse 18 ("little children") can be taken to mark a new beginning. Again, the Common Lectionary avoids the harsh language of controversy, as the discussion that leads up to verse 18 is omitted altogether.

That harsher language is, however, a closer reflection or imaging of the actual character of our society, or of the modern world, than we like to admit. In preaching from this text one might well consider not only the reality of murderousness as an

91

intention of the heart but the reality of murder itself. In America we live in a society plagued by murder, one in which the leading cause of death among young men of certain ages and ethnic groups is murder. Thousands upon thousands of Americans are murdered each year, from children in cribs to the elderly in their homes. To inveigh against the lovelessness of murderers may be futile, but can the preacher say nothing about the murderousness of our society? At every level, urban criminal through urban executive, our culture is permeated by the deification of wealth, power, sex, and status. The pursuit of all these goals stands in blatant contradiction to the New Testament commandment of love. This is so obviously true that it is too seldom said, or it is sometimes said by media preachers whose own lives seem to testify to the deification of these secular gods. No wonder that our society, in which love is cynically viewed as a foolish sentiment that may stand in the way of such unworthy goals as the world worships, is plagued not only by murderousness but by murder itself.

When one looks at the international scene, the same kinds of murderousness and murder are found. Our common human self-interests have motivated world leaders to seek nonviolent ways of dealing with disputes between nuclear powers. At the same time, the level of violence in struggles that stop short of declared war between sovereign states increases dramatically. The areas in which there has been an acceleration of such violence in recent years are too numerous to mention. The end of the Cold War does not seem likely to improve matters. Killing is characterized as terrorism or murder, as freedom-fighting or self-defense, depending on one's perspective. From the standpoint of the New Testament, however, it is all murder. And it is a universal phenomenon. Jews and Moslems murder one another in the Near East; Hindus and Buddhists in Sri Lanka; Christians in Ireland. We too easily take the language about murder in 1 John 3:12–15 to be symbolic or metaphorical when it is actually a quite accurate description of what we see going on around us. Want of love leads to hate, which expresses itself in murder. Murder is avenged by murder, and the cycle goes on.

1 John 3:19–24
We Shall Know That We Are of the Truth: Christian Reassurance

The motif of reassurance, which has been in the background since the antichrists were mentioned (2:18), now emerges into the foreground just before the Antichrist is mentioned once more (see 4:1–3). Although this dominant motif is quite clear, exactly what is meant is more difficult to determine. Apparently a situation is envisioned in which a believer's guilt, not sin, needs to be overcome ("whenever our hearts condemn us;" v. 20). Whether such guilt would have been aroused by the opponents, with their false teaching and specious claims, is not said. But in view of the fact that such opponents figure in the succeeding, as well as the previous, discussion, this is not unlikely. However that may be, it is plain enough that John regards the assurance that God (who "is greater than our hearts") offers, together with the believer's knowledge of his own deeds of love (cf. 3:18), as more than capable of overcoming the kind of guilt of which he speaks. The "by this" of verse 19 may look back to verse 18, as well as forward. That John appeals to external and objective standards or realities is significant: deeds of love actually done and God himself (v. 20). They have an overriding authority and are therefore able to reassure believers when they experience self-doubt or feel self-condemned. God's knowledge and the spoken reassurance that God knows can override believers' own uncertainties and doubt about their status.

Probably verses 21–22 have no consequential relationship to what precedes except that a different and happier situation is envisioned. Perhaps the thoughts expressed here are only too simple and obvious. If our hearts do not condemn us, if we do not suffer from a burden of guilt, fine! God gives those who do his will whatever they ask. The latter statement may present problems for those who have not received from God what they asked; yet it is clearly grounded in the thought and sayings of Jesus in the Gospel of John (14:13; 15:16; 16:23; etc.). The key

93

to this difficult statement is apparently to be found in keeping God's commandments and doing what pleases him. People who are thus attuned to God's will find their prayers answered. The fundamental message, however, is that those who obey God and live in love with their fellows are acceptable and pleasing to God, no matter what they feel. If they feel condemned or guilty, they may rely on God's knowledge and ability to over-rule doubt or guilt. If they do not feel such doubt or guilt, their confidence before God is perfectly proper, as befits those who obey his commandments and please him.

No sooner has John spoken of commandments in the plural than he switches to the singular, "commandment" (v. 23). Yet there are actually two, one theological or confessional and the other ethical: believe in the name of God's Son Jesus Christ and love one another. We are by now quite familiar with the love commandment (2:7–8; 3:11); the command to believe in the name of God's Son Jesus Christ is in that form new, although not unanticipated, in 1 John. (On believing in his *name,* see John 1:12; 2:23; 3:18; 20:31; 1 John 5:13.) Actually, this is the first time in 1 John that we have read of *believing* in Jesus Christ. Hereto-fore, John has spoken of *confessing* the Son. The formula "the name of Jesus" (or "the Lord Jesus") is quite frequent in the Book of Acts (e.g., 2:38; 3:16; 4:12; 10:48; 19:5) and is found also in Paul (e.g., 1 Cor. 1:2; 5:4). Evidently it was common Christian parlance. Because this is a basic affirmation of Christian belief, we should not be surprised to find that it contains language widespread in the New Testament.

Believing and even confessing Jesus are not, however, the principal ways of relating to him according to 1 John. Although obviously the initial and decisive step is to believe, and it is imperative to confess properly, *to abide* is the usual way of expressing the Christian's relationship to Jesus in 1 John (2:6; 2:24, 27–28; 3:6; cf. John 15:4–10). Here the mutual abiding of the believer and Jesus (or God) is the result of keeping his commandment (v. 24). Whether the pronouns in verse 24 refer to God or Christ is actually not entirely clear, but it does not make a great deal of difference to whom they refer, for John speaks interchangeably of the abiding or indwelling of the Christian with God or Christ, or both.

94 Finally, John invokes the Spirit as guarantor of the knowl-edge or awareness of this abiding. Given the role of the Spirit *(paraklētos)* in the Gospel, this is exactly what we might ex-

pect (cf. John 14:10–17, 25–26; 15:26–27; 16:7–15). It is only surprising that the Spirit does not play a larger role in 1 John. Commentators have remarked on what seems to be a less developed concept of the Spirit in the Epistle as compared with the Gospel. In all probability, this has something to do with the fact that within the Johannine community false claims have been made in the name of the Spirit (4:1–3), so that it becomes necessary to test the Spirits (or prophets speaking in the name of the Spirit) to see which is of God. Nevertheless, the reality of the Spirit remains important, and at this point John invokes the Spirit's presence as guarantor of the knowledge that Christians have, specifically the knowledge that God, through Christ, abides in them. (On the role of the Spirit in early Christianity, see also Acts 2:1–4; Gal. 3:2–5; 4:6–7; Rom. 8:13–17.) Our pericope thus ends on a note of the strong reassurance available to the Christian from God through the Holy Spirit.

In considering what this passage teaches, there is a certain danger in moving from the more or less forensic language of John ("condemn") to the modern psychological connotations ("guilt") that we have invoked. Yet the interpretation of the gospel means moving from the language and conceptuality of the ancients to parallel or analogous language of our own day, taking into consideration our different ways of viewing and understanding ourselves and the world in which we live. Given the underlying motif or purpose of reassurance that emerges at many points in the letter and the clear expression of such an intention in this passage, it is necessary and helpful to employ language that we use of psychological states or states of consciousness, to explain the text. John is plainly talking about how Christians may find reassurance in the face of the doubt, self-recrimination, or guilt that may arise within them. Quite possibly such a state of mind as John has in view was incited or triggered by the claims of the opponents, who always seem to lurk behind his writing. But whatever the cause, its reality as a state of mind cannot be doubted.

John's invocation of obedience as a way of reassuring ourselves is of central importance (the "by this" of v. 19 referring back to loving in deed and truth in v. 18). The God who commands accepts obedience to his commands as testimony to our belonging to the truth, and the genuineness of that obedience

95

is attested in concrete acts of love, not just in talking about love. John clarifies both the nature of obedience and its ground. The ground of obedience is God himself, who is "greater than our hearts" (the seat of consciousness and conscience) and as such is also the ground or basis of the possibility of reassurance. What God knows and reassures us of transcends our consciousness, even our conscience, so that in moments of self-accusation we may fall back upon him. The nature of obedience is twofold (v. 23). It is obedience to the love commandment, but that obedience presupposes, is based upon, belief "in the name of his Son Jesus Christ," that is, belief in the effective, saving work of Jesus Christ as God's Son, his word. John understands belief at once as faith and right confession, and as obedience to the essential meaning of Jesus Christ's message and mission, which is mutual love. It is not as if the two could be separated. There is no valid faith apart from such obedience (1:6; 2:9–11), but such obedience cannot exist apart from knowledge, faith, and confession of Christ.

The question of whether such obedient love could possibly exist where the gospel of Jesus Christ has never been preached or heard—or before it was preached and heard—is one that does not appear on John's horizon. Christian apologists and patristic theologians begin to consider such questions. In the New Testament the assumption reigns that Old Testament worthies who were obedient to God's revelation were fully acceptable to him. Beyond this the earliest Christian writers whose testimonies appear in the New Testament do not speculate. They are concerned with the proclamation of the gospel and the state of believers and the church.

The Common Lectionary lesson for the Fourth Sunday in Easter (cycle C) affords a good basis for preaching (i.e., 3:18–24). Although RSV, with the Nestle-Aland Greek New Testament, begins a new paragraph with verse 19, the Lectionary (and NRSV) division is defensible, particularly if, as we have maintained, the "by this" of verse 19 also looks back to verse 18.

As we have just observed, this text affords the preacher an opportunity to explore and explain the inner dynamic of John's thought. Not only does the connection between theology and ethics, faith and obedience, come into play but also their integral relationship to the important motif and purpose of reassurance. A vacuous kind of reassurance may be easy to come by.

The sort offered here by John finds its basis beyond the believer, in God, his faithfulness and knowledge, and in actual obedience to his command. John takes account of the vulnerability of Christian consciousness, and conscience, and thus does not ground reassurance in religious feeling or a confidence generated from within. If we have no such problem (vv. 21–22), then that is good and as it should be; there is then certainly no need to arouse such feelings of guilt and vulnerability. Quite the contrary.

Historically, and in our own practical experience, it is not the careless Christian, but more often the carefully conscientious one, who is plagued with a sense of guilt and inadequacy. Its origins may lie in genetic makeup, biochemical imbalance, or early childhood, for all we know. There is a kind of preaching and Christian life-style that, in effect, preys upon such feelings. Better to keep them alive if they keep people coming to church! There are various religious nostrums intended to address such spiritual illness, most of which are designed to produce better feelings, whether by appeal to the hearer to revive and renew his spiritual life or by reference to the truths of psychology. Christian preaching need not disparage the value of spiritual discipline or genuine psychological insights. Yet its primary ground, or point of reference, is neither, but rather an appeal to the gospel and the God of the gospel whose reassurance comes first of all through the announcement of the message that was from the beginning, that is, the message that God is light (1:5), and that he is, gives, and commands love (4:8; 3:1, 11).

1 John 4:1–6
Test the Spirits: Orthodoxy Versus Heresy in the Johannine Churches

This is an important section theologically because it indicates the existence of what we would call heresy and at the same time raises the problem of whether and how the claim to speak by inspiration of the Spirit may be justified and tested.

John now warns the readers again about his opponents and their false views and claims. Presumably he here refers to the separatists about whom we have already read (2:18–19), and his description of them and their views sheds light on what he has written (2:22–23). In both cases he decries them by accusing them either of being the Antichrist (2:18) or of representing his spirit (4:3). At first (4:1–3), it is not entirely obvious that he is describing these people, or, indeed, any people at all. He speaks rather of testing spirits. Yet the necessity of testing the spirits stems from the fact that many false prophets have gone into the world (v. 1). Obviously, the false prophets of whom John speaks claim Spirit inspiration, and it is precisely that claim that must be tested. Later, when he refers to "them" (v. 4), it is quite clear that certain people are meant, for "spirit" *(pneuma)* is neuter in Greek, and the pronoun used for "them" is masculine, referring to persons. Moreover, in verses 4 and 5 John makes entirely plain the fact that he is writing about people who are in the world, of the world, and receiving the favorable attention of the world. What is said here complements the description of them in 2:19.

The call to test the spirits demands that the author should say how, or by what means, the spirits are to be tested. He promptly does so, stating a positive criterion by which one may discern the Spirit of God or the claim to possess that Spirit. It is a theological or confessional criterion (v. 2): the confession that Jesus Christ has come in the flesh is valid and true, authenticating the claim to possess the Spirit. The negative criterion is then stated (v. 3); but a problem arises because the false, or inadequate, confession is not fully the obverse of the positive. That is, the spirit that is not of God is said not to confess Jesus rather than not to confess "that Jesus Christ has come in the flesh." The text as it stands could mean that the spirit or confession of every non-Christian is not of God, since by definition the nonbeliever, whether Jew or Gentile, does not confess Jesus. This is obviously true on John's terms. Yet such an interpretation is hardly intelligible in the context of 1 John, and in this passage particularly, where the overall question or issue is the claim of authentic Spirit possession or inspiration within the Christian church. How is it to be validated? Not to confess Jesus may simply be shorthand for the obverse of the positive confession and criterion. Significantly, the false confession is a failure to confess Jesus rather than Jesus Christ. Do the opponents somehow confess Christ without affirming, or adequately affirming, Jesus? Apparently, some such position is in view. Sim-

98

ply not to confess Jesus Christ at all would put these folk outside the church and outside the range of the author's concern.

That such failure to confess Jesus means failure to confess his coming in the flesh, that is, his manhood or humanity, would seem to be confirmed by 2 John 7, where the Antichrist and deceiver is said precisely not to "confess that Jesus Christ has come in the flesh" (NRSV). Even if one regards 2 John as the work of another, later author (a position this commentary does not embrace), the author of that letter seems to have construed 1 John 4:3a as having this meaning. In addition, the heavy stress laid on the physical visibility, audibility, and tangibility of Jesus in the prologue of 1 John lends weight to this interpretation. The prologue is intended to emphasize the proper interpretation of the incarnation in the face of any who would dilute it. An early textual variant, found in some ancient Latin manuscripts and Greek patristic authors, reads in 4:3a "annuls" (or "dissolves") Jesus instead of "does not confess Jesus." Brown argues that this is the original reading and indeed it fits the context well. The preponderance of Greek manuscripts, however, read "does not confess," so most commentators shy away from the reading "annul" (Greek *luei;* Latin *solvit*), even though it likely catches the meaning of the author more precisely than what he wrote!

To sum up, although certainty about the historical situation of 1 John is unattainable, it is not hard to imagine what has been going on. A plausible, and even probable, scenario can be constructed. Christian prophets claiming the authority of the Spirit (or of Christ) have been addressing the community. Whether in Spirit-inspired utterance or otherwise, they have espoused a false Christology. That is, they have not espoused the necessary and proper confession that Jesus has come in the flesh (cf. 2 John 7). Thus, they do not confess Jesus. (Whether they espouse the kind of docetic Christology known from later Christian sources is hard to say.) The Spirit of God inspires a valid confession of Jesus, and by its absence one can recognize the false spirits. When John calls these false spirits the spirit of the antichrist (4.3), we are immediately able to confirm that they are identical with the separatists to whom he has already referred (2:18–19). At the same time we infer that the denial that Jesus is the Christ mentioned earlier (2:22) must mean that they deny that Jesus is the Christ come in the flesh.

99

We have already seen how John invokes the apocalyptic

figure of the antichrist (viz., 2:18–19) to characterize the false prophets whose doctrine and claim of authority he rejects. Their presence suggests that it is the last hour (2:18). Now John refers to the community's knowledge that the antichrist is coming (the traditional expectation) in order to say that "it is in the world already" (4:3). This statement obviously also suggests the nearness of the end time. Now John can go on to identify the antichrists and their false confession with the world that stands over against God (cf. 2:15–17). In John's dualistic mode of thought, being "of the world" (4:5) is the polar opposite of being "of God" (4:4), just as the antichrist is the polar opposite of the Christ. The fact that the world listens to John's opponents is not surprising and proves them not right but wrong! There are ultimately only two possibilities: the world or God. Jesus Christ and his true disciples, particularly the author himself, are of God. The antichrist(s), the opponents, and by implication any who may follow them, are of the world. (The apparent policy of the NRSV translators to render *ek* consistently here and elsewhere with "from" does not seem to me to be an entirely happy one. "From" can imply separation and distance, whereas "of" connotes origin and nature, which are obviously at stake here.)

The final statements of this paragraph (v. 6) may seem the height of arrogance. "We" here means the author and those who are associated with him or follow him. He is the apostolic authority for this community of Christians, the one who knows the one who was from the beginning, that is, Jesus. Who the author was we can never know for certain although ancient tradition identifies him as John, the disciple of the Lord, the Beloved Disciple of the Gospel. Whoever he may have been, he bases his authority not on any particular personal gift or capacity but on this relationship with Jesus, who was from the beginning. He obviously has no doubt about the reality of his relationship with Jesus, even though its exact character is hidden from us. The opening lines of the prologue speak of a sure and certain seeing and contact but tantalize us with the first-person plural pronoun "we" (cf. John 1:1–18; 21:24). Does the author mean himself, who along with others was contemporary with Jesus, or does he mean that he stands in solidarity with an earlier generation of eyewitnesses? In any event, his confident assertion is based on the reality of Jesus himself.

100

Because of the certainty of this witness, those who know God reveal themselves as such in hearing the author ("us"),

listening to him, and those who are not of God identify themselves by their inattention to him. This may seem all too simple
a method for identifying the spirits of truth and error, but we
should remember that in John's view the criterion is really
whether or not one confesses Jesus properly. He and those
associated with him do this.

It would be understandable, but probably mistaken, to attempt to derive a Christian teaching about the Holy Spirit from
this pericope. In a certain sense the Spirit—or, rather, the claim
to possess the Spirit—is the problem. The community must
distinguish between the spirits, to discern the true Spirit among
false claims of Spirit possession or inspiration. Nevertheless, the
church lives by the Spirit, something John does not think of
denying. There are, however, better scriptural and Johannine
bases for the development of a Christian doctrine of the Spirit.

What this text does demonstrate is the limitations inherent
in the ministry of the Spirit. The Spirit does not work in a
vacuum or independently of any other authority in the church.
In questions of doctrine or discipline, claims of spiritual inspiration do not have an overriding authority. The issue of the
authority of the Spirit came to a head in the Montanist controversy of the second century and later as the followers of Mon-
tanus in effect claimed such authority for their prophecies,
basing their claims on the Spirit-Paraclete sayings of Jesus in the
farewell discourses of the Gospel of John. Those sayings of Jesus
in fact extend the revelation of Jesus into the future of the
postresurrection church. On the other hand, they make clear
that this revelation belongs to Jesus. Set as they are in the
context of the Gospel and put on the lips of Jesus, these sayings
can be interpreted as not only extending the revelation of Jesus
but tying it to Jesus and thus preventing it from floating free in
any direction. Jesus is the test of any claim to possess the Spirit.
In fact, Jesus is the standard to whom 1 John constantly refers,
as the author insists upon obedience to him as well as to the
right confession of him as having come in the flesh. Neither 1
John nor the Gospel of John conveys nearly so much tradition
of the historical Jesus as do the Synoptics. Yet both capture the
essential Jesus, who appeared as a human being at a specific
time in history, commanding people to love one another. Any-   101
one who denies either aspect of this revelation, by failing to
acknowledge Jesus' humanity or by hating rather than loving,

cannot claim to possess his Spirit and to walk in the light. That person is instead in darkness and death.

Because the point of this passage is Jesus' humanity, we should consider what this affirmation means for Christian teaching, specifically Christology. The ancient church struggled to express the nature and meaning of Jesus in terms that were not only intelligible but faithful to, and expressive of, the revelation and salvation that it had received. The Council of Nicaea (A.D. 325) thus affirmed that God himself was present or incarnate in Jesus Christ, not some subordinate divine being. Accordingly, he was said to be begotten, not made, and coexistent with God the Father before creation.

This affirmation left the matter of Jesus' humanity undefined, if in one way or another assumed by most Christians. It remained for the Council of Chalcedon (A.D. 451) to affirm the balance between the Godhead and humanity in declaring Jesus Christ to be at once fully God and fully human. This affirmation laid down the boundaries for the future development of Christology and doctrine without anticipating all the issues that might arise and without fully taking account of how divinity and humanity might coexist uniquely in one person. The Monophysite heresy, which dissolved Jesus' humanity into his divinity, was popular and in one form or another remains so. It has proven an easy and tempting course to regard the human Jesus as the shell or form in which lives a divine being who is not subject to the exigencies of human existence. Precisely the Johannine doctrine of the preexistence of Christ seems to justify such a view.

Nevertheless, it is John, in the Gospel and especially in the First Epistle, who insists more strongly than any other New Testament writer on the visibility and palpability of God in the truly human Jesus. Along with this goes his insistence that Jesus should be obeyed and followed. As he walked, so we should walk (2:6). Belief in Jesus' genuine humanity is the underlying presupposition, the sine qua non, of the primitive and continuing conviction that the Christian is obligated and able to walk as Jesus himself walked. Classical Christian belief has two sides that are always held together. If Jesus is not truly God, he cannot bring salvation to us; if he is not truly human, this salvation cannot be effectual for us nor is it relevant to us. This latter aspect is epitomized in Jesus' death.

102

According to the New Testament and basic Christian doctrine, the death of Jesus is important both because of its saving effect and because it is motivated by and expresses Jesus' (and God's) love for humankind. We have already seen how in both these respects Jesus' death occupies an indispensable role in the Gospel and letters of John: It accomplishes salvation and is the ultimate expression of love. Moreover, Jesus' death is the proof of his humanity. Only as a human being could he really die; thus in antiquity, especially in Gnostic doctrine, denial of Jesus' humanity was accompanied by denial of the reality of his death. He only seemed to die. Yet, as the orthodox Fathers of the church objected, if he only seemed to die a human death, how could his sacrifice be for us, and how could it guide and motivate us to show a similar love for our fellows (cf. John 15:12–13; 1 John 3:16)?

The possibilities for preaching from this text are, of course, rich. Certainly one could preach a didactic sermon on the Christology explicit, and implicit, in this passage, as we have just outlined it. Docetic Christologies, in which Jesus only seems to be human (Greek: *dokein,* "to seem"), have seldom been lacking in popular Christianity, and versions of such Christology abound still. The Divine Redeemer is all too easily shorn of the basic elements of humanity, often by those who think in doing so they honor him. This happens not so often as a process of abstract theological thought as one of piety and practical discipleship. Jesus is no longer with us and leading us but is above us and irrelevant to us. In a day when "liberal" has become a kind of semiotic or verbal scapegoat, it is important that the authentic christological and ethical aspects of an older evangelical liberalism not be lost.

Other parts or aspects of this text present valid homiletical possibilities. The observation that the world follows after the heretics ("listens to them") is more than a condemnation of their teaching by associating it with the darkness of this world. It is also a concession that these opponents have attracted a substantial following. Brown suggests that they represent a wing of the Johannine community that has broken off and moved in the wrong direction theologically, perhaps taking a majority with them. Probably he is correct although we can scarcely know for sure. Perhaps just the combination of a claimed spiritual inspiration and docetic Christology rendered their movement popular. If so, that has happened more than

103

once in the past and continues to happen today. Without resorting to a negative kind of preaching, the preacher can emulate 1 John in emphasizing authentic, orthodox confession and obedience to Jesus as the necessary hallmarks of Christian faith and discipleship. Otherworldliness, whether in Christian or non-Christian forms, has always attracted an audience, perhaps because it affords an all-too-easy escape from this world and its problems (cf. John 17:15). It must be confronted with the one who was from the beginning and who became truly human, and with what he commanded.

REFLECTION:
Spiritual Authority in the Johannine Community

Behind the controversy about true and false spirits reflected in 1 John 4:1–6, there lies the phenomenon of spiritual authority and the problems the exercise of such authority can engender in the church. In all likelihood we can trace the development of these problems in the Gospel of John and the Book of Revelation. In the Gospel of John, Jesus repeatedly promises the disciples the gift of the Spirit (e.g., 14:15–17) and tells them that this Spirit or Counselor will teach them the things they will need to know (14:26; 16:12–15). In fact, the disciples' deficiency in understanding during Jesus' historic ministry seems to reflect directly the fact that the Spirit has not yet come (7:39; 12:16). They did not understand, not because they were culpable, but because they could not in the nature of the case understand until Jesus had been glorified and the Spirit interpreted matters for them. John's Gospel is based upon the perceived and received power and knowledge given by the Spirit to believers. Quite possibly the words of Jesus in the Gospel of John, so different from those found in the Synoptic Gospels, or even in Paul's letters, are a product of—or somehow related to—this kind of spiritual inspiration. The importance of the Spirit for inspiration and understanding is well attested in other New Testament books (Acts 1:8; 2:1–4, 17–18, 33, 38; Rom. 8:1–17). In fact, the New Testament generally makes clear that only after the resurrection and with the Spirit's inspiration do the followers of Jesus comprehend what has taken place among them.

In the Revelation to John particularly, Christ is portrayed as speaking directly to the churches through the Spirit. In other words, what is portrayed as happening in Revelation chapters 1—3 is not unlike what the Gospel of John would lead us to expect. Jesus has promised further, direct revelation, and now he delivers. (The tone of the revelation is negative in the Book of Revelation, not positive as the Gospel implies, but that is because of the behavior of the churches in question.) The voice who speaks to John at the beginning of his revelation is, when John looks, described as a heavenly, perhaps apocalyptic, figure (Rev. 1:12–16). This figure is based on descriptions found in the late biblical prophetic literature, particularly Daniel, where we find a "son of man" (Dan. 7:13), just as we do in Revelation (1:13) as well as in the Synoptic Gospels (Mark 14:62). That this figure is the heavenly Christ, not God or the Spirit, is, however, made very clear in Revelation 1:17–18: "I died, and behold I am alive for evermore." It is this Christ who speaks to the churches of Ephesus, Smyrna, Pergamum, Thyatira, Sardis, Philadelphia, and Laodicea in the seven letters of Revelation 1—3. Christ dictates the letters, transcribed by John, which are addressed to the angels of the seven churches. The words of Christ, who speaks in the first person singular, are, however, repeatedly described as words that the Spirit says to the churches (2:7, 11, 17, etc.). In effect, the words of the heavenly Christ are words of the Spirit. This equivalency is very much like what we find also in the Gospel of John.

A generation earlier, Spirit-inspired speech seems to have created problems in Pauline churches. First Corinthians 12—14 attests the existence of such problems, and more specifically, we read of a situation similar to 1 John 4:1–3 in 1 Corinthians 12:1–3 (cf. also 12:10 and 14:32). There the proper Christian confession that Jesus is Lord is the mark of inspiration by the Holy Spirit, whereas a statement such as "Jesus be cursed!" cannot be so inspired. Whether there were actually people in Corinth claiming the inspiration of the Spirit for such a statement is at least doubtful, but whether or not there were, the principle Paul enunciates is clear enough: The claim to possess the Spirit cannot warrant statements that obviously run counter to Christian truth. In fact, earlier in his career Paul had already warned his readers, just in the context of admonishing them neither to quench the Spirit nor to despise prophesying, to "test everything" (1 Thess. 5:21). Also 1 Timothy 4:1 has Paul warn the faithful of deceitful spirits and false doctrines that are to appear, and the Little Apocalypse warns disciples of false Christs and false prophets (Mark 13:22). The early church lived by the Spirit but had to establish criteria by which genuine and false claims to Spirit inspiration could be identified. Thus in 1 John and elsewhere, right doctrine or right confession becomes a means of validating, or invalidating, claims to speak with the inspiration or authority of the Spirit.

1 John 4:7–12
Love Is of God: The Theology of Love

This paragraph is one of the most eloquent statements about love in the Johannine literature, as well as in the New Testament as a whole. As such it is perhaps less famous than 1 Corinthians 13. But in fact it is a more adequate theological discussion about the origin of love than Paul's famous poem of praise, which has been popular among Christians, as well as others, perhaps because it extols the importance and character of love over against narrowly religious qualities or claims. John, on the other hand, gives a distinctly Christian explanation of the origin and human motivation of love, one that has become a classical model for theology and ethics. Appropriately, John begins by addressing his readers as beloved (cf. 4:1), recipients of love. Obviously, they are beloved by the author, but, as we shall soon see, also beloved of God, and this becomes evident in the way this paragraph unfolds.

That love is of God is the basic premise of Christian faith and theology. Therefore, the one who loves demonstrates that she or he is born of God and knows God (v. 7). These statements should not be taken out of context as if they were applicable universally apart from God's revelation in Jesus. They are addressed to the Christian community and are intended to be understood on the basis of God's revelation in Christ. Those who claim that revelation demonstrate their rebirth and knowledge of God by loving their fellows. Whether any or all manifes-

106

tations of love demonstrate such rebirth and knowledge is a question the author really does not entertain. Yet failure to love invalidates any claim to know God (v. 8). That God is love is not an exhaustive description of God but a statement of how God manifests himself to us. Because God manifests himself to us as love, not to love is in the very nature of the case not to know him (v. 8). This comment is obviously aimed at certain members of the church, but it could be extended to all human beings, even if its positive counterpart may not be.

The general statements about love and God (4:7–8) are now brought into relation to the Christian revelation of who God is and what love is (vv. 9–10). God defines the nature of love by giving his Son (v. 10). It is important to notice the relation of this statement to John 3:16, which seems to be pre-supposed. Yet 1 John does not say that God loved the world, but speaks of the love of God being made manifest (RSV) or revealed (NRSV) "among us" (presumably Christians) by the sending of the Son into the world "so that we might live through him." (Nevertheless, in 4:14 Jesus is called the Savior of the world.) Very important in John 3:16 and here is the self-sacrificial character of God's love, which is bound up with the faith that God has sent, in the sense of given up, his Son. This is, of course, closely related to Christ's giving up his life for his friends (John 15:12–13).

The very definition of love turns upon God's sending, i.e., giving up, his Son for the expiation of sins (v. 10). (The NRSV has "atoning sacrifice" rather than "expiation.") Because Jesus deals with and does away with sin, we live through him (v. 9). Knowledge of God's love is given in God's own deed. Particularly important is the fact that God has taken the initiative. The definition of love proceeds from God: "not that we loved God but that he loved us." Again, the love of God is not conceived in the abstract but based upon his concrete, historical deed in the appearance and death of Jesus Christ. One could say the love of God is an interpretation of the death of Jesus, or that the early Christians inferred from Jesus' death that God sent him, out of love, for the purpose of dealing with sin (cf. Rom. 5:8; Gal. 2:20). Historically speaking, such explanations of the doctrine make sense as accounting for the genesis of the idea. Yet in John's view the truth of his interpretation as the necessary ex- 107 planation and meaning of what happened belongs to the heart and essence of the gospel. It is not one possible interpretation out of several that might make sense historically; it is the correct and adequate interpretation. In what sense, or to what extent, it may be obligatory for the Christian of this or any period to share John's understanding is a matter well worth pondering.

Next, John lays down the fundamental premise of Christian ethics (v. 11) as if it were axiomatic (v. 12), as, indeed, it was for him, and as it has become for most Christians ever since. John expects the logic of his assertion to be compelling as he brings to expression what would come to be recognized as an apt summation of the New Testament message. John will explore in the remainder of the chapter why the move from the love of God to our obligation to love one another is compelling. Christian moralists have often reflected on the rationale for our loving one another that John sets forth here. For Christians generally, John's move seems natural and obvious. He has prepared the reader for it by describing God's love with specific reference to God's sending of his Son to death for our salvation. Communion with God, who is love in his self-manifestation, requires that one share in this love by loving others.

God is accessible to us only as we love (v. 12). The theme of seeing God is introduced in order to make this point (cf. John 1:18). In the believer, as well as in God's historic revelation in Jesus, God's reality manifests itself as love. Apart from love shared, whether by God for us or by ourselves for one another, it is meaningless to inquire about God's reality or being. John will dwell upon this theme in the next section. The repeated statement that God is love (4:8, 16) should not be taken to mean that God is love in the sense that God is a feeling, an attitude, an intention, or even an action on the part of human beings. John had made it amply clear that the existence and will of God and his action in love toward us through Jesus Christ are the grounds for our knowledge of God's love, and that God's love is the basis for our obligation to love one another, which is so succinctly expressed in the love commandment. Does God then exist apart from love? That is a good question, and the answer is not as easy as it might appear. Certainly God exists apart from love understood in purely human terms (above). Whether God exists apart from the creative, sustaining, and redemptive will that governs the universe, or whether God's existence can be perceived apart from our acceptance of, and belief in, that will as having its origin in him is another matter.

Obviously 1 John 4:7–12 is a classic text dealing with a central Christian teaching and concern. No Christian teacher has spoken more directly and eloquently about the origin and meaning of love, not even Paul in 1 Corinthians 13. Here the theological indicative grounds the moral imperative. Because God loves, we ought to love, not only God, but also one another. Of course, the person whom God loves will reciprocate that love. That goes without saying. The perfecting of love in us (v. 12) cannot mean anything less than that our love toward God, as well as other human beings, will be perfected. That John gives voice to this distinctly Christian concept of love against the background of a situation in which he finds that some claiming the name of Christ do not profess or practice love does not make what he says less significant.

If what he writes reflects a concrete and specific set of circumstances, he stands in solidarity with us, for we can never escape our historicity, the fact that we live within certain constraints and relationships. Timeless truths may be irrelevant for those like us who live within time. Only truths uttered under the conditions of our existence are relevant to it. The grammar of Christian confession and obedience is set out quite plainly here, and in such a way that it may be learned and applied in many different settings of time and place. John's statements have an elemental, as well as elementary, quality.

The priority of God's love as the meaning of Jesus' ministry and death is basic to Christian belief and confession. To put it differently, the perception of God's love in Jesus' ministry and death gives rise to Christian confession. Historically speaking, Christian belief arose out of such a perception of God's love and consists of that perception, so that where it is lacking, one cannot speak of Christian faith at all.

It follows from the perception of God's love that those who know love know God and obey him, and this obedience in turn finds expression in love: love for God but particularly love for one's fellows. As God's love is no abstraction but consists in the giving up of his Son, so the believer's love is not merely an emotion or attitude but consists of meaningful deeds (3:17–18). Apart from such deeds the very claim to love becomes vacuous.

The concluding note about the perfecting of love (v. 12) has attracted the attention of theologians as well as exegetes. The Greek word translated "perfected" *(teleioun)* also has the meaning of being brought to completion in the sense of reaching a goal. Candidates for ministry in the Wesleyan tradition are asked whether they expect to be perfected in love in this life and are supposed to be able to give a positive answer. Aside from the fact that whatever John means by perfected applies to all Christians, not just clergy, the statement and its application present problems. Obviously, John believes that Christ does away with sin and that the Christian should and can be free of sin (3:4–10). On the other hand, he deprecates the claim that one is sinless or has not sinned (1:8, 10). We have already observed this tension within the letter.

Quite possibly, the too-narrow interpretation of perfection as sinlessness, not uncommon in the Wesleyan tradition, has created problems unnecessarily. What the text actually says is that mutual love insures God's presence ("God abides in us") and the perfection or completion of his love among us. The Greek conditional clause of verse 12 is a future condition, expressing a kind of inconclusiveness about the fulfillment of the action of loving: "If ever we love one another. . . ." Significantly, the if-clause of the preceding statement (v. 11) is a simple condition that suggests no uncertainty but presumes a fact: "Since God so loved us. . . ." The issue is therefore not whether God loves us in Christ—God does—but whether we shall love one another. Insofar as we love one another, God abides in us and his love is perfected, in the sense of completed, in us. God's love is then brought to perfection or completion in us to the extent that we love our fellow believers.

Once again John focuses on the Christian community, as he does throughout the Gospel as well as the letters. While this focus need not be construed as a limitation of love, so that the Christian today has no responsibility to love those outside the church, it is nonetheless significant. Of course, we all too easily approach texts such as this with the assumption that relationships within the Christian community are going to be smoother, easier, less conflictual, than those without. This was not true in the first generation or in John's time, and it obviously has not always been the case since. One need only look around to observe high levels of hostility within Christian churches. Oftentimes the structure of the tension is similar to what we find in the Johannine letters. On the one hand, there is the insistence on right confession, the definition of the faith. On the other, there is the obligation of love. Particularly within the Christian

110

community the two pose tensions or come into conflict, as they appear to do in 1 John. Shall we love someone who does not, in our view, utter the right confession?

The homiletical possibilities offered by this text scarcely need be named. Perhaps a certain danger should be cautioned against. The statement that God is love (cf. v. 16) must not be sentimentalized. As we have seen, it should be put into its literary—and theological—context. God's love is expressed in a person and an event in which God takes initiative (vv. 9–10). Human love, expressed in concrete acts (3:17–18), is the proper mode of receptivity to God's love (4:12).

The integral theological and ethical relationship between indicative (God's love for us) and imperative (our love for others) is the crux of this text. Valid preaching from it will overcome the moralizing that not only lacks theological basis but quickly becomes rather tiresome. One could scarcely preach from this pericope and fall into that sort of moralizing, particularly if the passage is treated as a whole, for the priority of God's love is set forth with unmistakable clarity (v. 10). While this priority may seem a truism for exegesis and theology, it bears reiteration from the pulpit. Not only is the priority of God's love and his initiative the heart of the Christian message, but this message is so strange to modern ears and so counter to modern expectations that it needs repeating even within the church. The perception of the world and society as a loveless place, and the interpretation of love in terms of individual emotion, not to mention erotic attraction, stand over against the message that is the gospel.

From a worldly perspective, the gospel's message of God's love is quite uncanny and unbelievable, a state of affairs that would not in the least surprise the author of 1 John. It belongs to the character of the world not to believe such an unworldly message. Does the message have any basis in a reality that is perceptible and real? Only in the reality of mutual human love. Such love becomes a possibility, not only a possibility but a necessity—a joyful necessity—as a response to God's love made manifest in the historical human Jesus. God's love is prior, but shared human love vindicates and validates the claim that God loves. It makes the message of God's love credible in witness to the world.

One need not, however, deny the genuineness of human

111

affection, human love, apart from the gospel message and our grateful response to it. It might be said that such love is inherently self-interested, but such a charge runs the risk of being doctrinaire and unfair. We do not have to first prove the world false in order that the gospel may be true. God's love in Jesus Christ and our responsive love become perceptible and credible because people already know what love means, know the necessity of it, and long for love's adequate reciprocity and fulfillment.

1 John 4:13–21
By This We Know We Abide in Him: Confessing and Loving

The love of God, demonstrated in the sending or giving of his Son, is the ground and basis for God's claim upon us, which we fulfill by abiding in that love as we love our fellows. This basic grammar of Christian confession and practice is expressed in a number of ways, with sometimes the indicative and at other times the imperative given precedence. As we have already been able to observe, 1 John's thought moves in a spiral-like formation, circling back on itself, rather than in a strict logical progression. Not that there is no logic in 1 John; there is a logic, as we have seen in the previous pericope.

The long pericope 4:13–21 is a kind of summation of Johannine themes, but there is a question as to whether it is a unity. RSV has it as a single paragraph. The current edition of the standard Nestle-Aland Greek New Testament, followed by the NRSV, begins a new paragraph with verse 16b. There were, of course, no paragraphs in the ancient manuscripts. The paragraphing of the RSV in effect sets off 4:13–21 as a summation, which is appropriate at this point. Most editions of the Greek text, as well as translations, agree that chapter 5 begins a separate unit of thought, although some commentators disagree. As a summation, 4:13–21 brings together the dominant themes, with verses, 13–16a emphasizing human witnessing, confessing, and assurance, and verses 16b–21 emphasizing the importance of human love. Thus the division into two paragraphs can be

112

justified. Both poles of Johannine thought, so to speak, the indic-ative and the imperative, are brought together.

At the outset (v. 13) the reassuring role of the Spirit is mentioned. Heretofore, claims to possess the Spirit have cre-ated problems (4:1–3), but the claims would not have been problematic had not the Johannine community emphasized the role of the Spirit. The Spirit reassures Christians of their mutual indwelling or abiding with God and Christ. Talk of a mystical union of Father, Son, Spirit, and Christian goes somewhat beyond what is said in the text but is not misleading. Johannine language is distinctive at this point, but not entirely unique (cf. Gal. 2:20; 3:27–28). The gospel invites belief not only as assent but as participation in a new reality that God is bringing about (cf. 2 Cor. 5:17). The basis for the knowledge of this reality is the mission of the Son, whose ministry and death have been seen and attested (v. 14).

The appropriate response to the Son is belief and confes-sion, which are the condition and cause of God's abiding in the Christian (v. 15). Providing assurance or mutual abiding or in-dwelling is an important work of the Spirit (v. 13). We are again seeing a dominant motif of 1 John, which is to reassure the readers, the believing community, of their standing (v. 16a). Probably this reassurance was necessitated in the first instance by external threat, that is, by the separatists who had broken away from the community and taken many with them. Yet the basic structure or components of this reassurance—the deed of God's love, the testimony borne to it, the work of the Spirit—are not dependent upon this or any particular set of historical circumstances. They are ever present and available to the Christian. Thus in 4:13–16a the grounds of reassurance are reit-erated and summarized; God is the ultimate ground of the believer's status and confidence.

In verse 16b (which begins a new paragraph in the Greek text and in the NRSV) the other side of this reassurance appears. If verses 13–16a reiterate the indicative of the gospel, verses 16b–21 restate the imperative. Yet "imperative" is now some-thing of a misnomer, for it implies a demand to be fulfilled, hence the possibility of nonfulfillment and the failure of expec-tation and hope. What follows, however, is not so much a de-mand as the possibility of reassurance. It is precisely love toward one's fellows, in obedience to Jesus' example and com-mand, that constitutes such reassurance (vv. 16b–18). Precisely

113

in loving we know that we are loved. The reality of love is not an intellectual abstraction; it is an existential attitude leading to concrete action (3:17–18; 4:20). Within that attitude and action lies the possibility, indeed the certainty, of reassurance. Only by abiding in love are Christians able to abide in God, and God in them, in a state of mutual indwelling.

John next describes how love effects reassurance (vv. 17–18) in statements that can, and perhaps should, be read on two levels. On the one level, love as obedience removes the fear of punishment for disobedience. On the other level, love as abandonment of self-interest and self-concern cuts the ground from under fear.

The perfecting or completion of love produces confidence in the day of judgment (v. 17). The perfecting of love comes about through following Christ, the *imitatio christi;* the reader is reminded of what has been said earlier about walking as Jesus walked (2:6). In both places the pronoun "he" obviously refers to Jesus, even though following strictly the syntactical rules of Greek, it would be taken to refer to God as the nearest antecedent. On the other hand, the demonstrative pronoun used, "that one" or "that man" *(ekeinos),* is ordinarily applied to Jesus. Clearly, the content of the statements makes clear that the reference is to Jesus. Thus the Christian is called upon to be like Jesus in the world. "In the world, but not of it" may seem a somewhat hackneyed slogan, but it expresses John's thought exactly. The follower of Jesus remains faithful to his calling in the world, even as Jesus did (cf. John 17:15). This faithfulness consists in obedience to Jesus, particularly the love commandment (John 14:15; 13:34; 1 John 2:7–11), even as Jesus was obedient to God's commands (cf. John 15:10). The love commandment is, in the Johannine view, the summation and epitome of all that Jesus taught. Faithfulness to Jesus removes any need to fear the day of judgment.

John's next two statements (v. 18) can be viewed as expanding upon verse 17. Love casts out fear of the judgment that will fall on the disobedient. It is noteworthy that John assumes a future judgment, even for Christians. Thus he agrees with Paul (2 Cor. 5:10); but there may be a tension with the Gospel of John, which sometimes places the believer already beyond judgment (5:24). Perhaps the situation of heresy and schism within the community has caused our author some second thoughts. The term for punishment (Greek: *kolasis*) otherwise occurs only in Matthew 25:46 ("eternal punishment"), where it obviously refers to eschatological punishment, which seems to be the meaning in our context. Whether a more profound understanding of the relationship of love and fear is also intended is uncertain, but such a relationship is at least suggested. That is, love, in its going out to the other and forgetfulness of self, leaves fear behind, trusting in God. Certainly in this sense the perfection or completion (v. 18) of love means, logically, the elimination of fear. Where love reigns, and fills one's being, there is no room for fear. In any case, the note of reassurance is sounded strongly.

Then comes a reiteration of the logic of Christian morality (v. 19): "We love, because he first loved us." John has said it previously (4:7–12) but never more succinctly. Here, as in his immediately preceding statements about love and fear, John uncovers a profound psychological truth even as he unfolds his theology. Love can be received only as it is shared. To be the object of love without sharing love with others may be theoretically possible, but it is self-corrupting, if not destructive, contradicting the character and defeating the purpose of loving. At the same time, God's love frees us from self-concern and thus enables us truly to love others. John does not now reflect on such matters, however, but moves immediately to a practical consequence (v. 20) and a reiteration of the old commandment (v. 21).

When John wants to underscore a point, he sometimes envisions an antagonist who says the opposite or acts falsely and then brands the one who speaks or acts in that way a liar. He does this here (v. 20), as he has in 1:8 (cf. 1:10). Quite possibly he has specific people in mind. The person who claims to love God while hating the brother can be described unequivocally in the framework of the Johannine dualism: "He is a liar." That is to say, he is opposed to the truth. Why? The answer is simple and obvious and brings a smile to the readers' lips, as once again John invokes the theme of seeing—or not seeing—God. The reality of the unseen God who is love is apprehended as we love one another (cf. 4:12), and the failure of love among those who see each other gives the lie to any claim of loving—or knowing—this unseen God. The symmetry of this statement (v. 20b) is a key to its beauty. At this point (vv. 20–21) the NRSV characteristically makes clear the more inclusive meaning; thus "brother or sister" is substituted for the RSV's "brother."

115

The person from whom we have the commandment that the one who loves God should love the brother and sister also (v. 21) is surely Jesus, although some manuscripts read "God," apparently because again according to Greek rules of syntax God should be the antecedent. Yet the Johannine reader knows that Jesus has given the love commandment, which by now has been referred or alluded to several times (cf. John 13:34; 1 John 2:7–8; 3:11). At this point we may also see a faint reflection of the synoptic tradition of the commandment to love God and neighbor (Mark 12:29–31 par., in which Jesus cites Deut. 6:4–5 and Lev. 19:18). Our author obviously knows the Gospel of John, or its constitutive traditions, well, but such reminiscences of the specifically synoptic tradition are very rare indeed.

As we have observed, John here reiterates major aspects of his teaching, first emphasizing once again the themes of God's love, the sending of the Son, and the assurance of the Spirit, then turning to the level of human relationships and stressing the indispensibility of mutual love, which is our proper response to God's love, providing reassurance and confidence that God's love is indeed given for us. In a sense, there is nothing new in this pericope; John says again what he has already said, but graphically and succinctly. His dismissal of the possibility of any love for God apart from human love is a classic formulation.

Whether this text as it is given in the RSV (all one paragraph) provides a unified basis for preaching, or for one sermon, is a legitimate question. Rich though it may be in Johannine themes, it is not found in the Common Lectionary. Inasmuch as there is a major turn from God's love to human love in the middle of verse 16, it might be wise to choose one or the other half of this text as the basis for a single sermon. On the other hand, as we can clearly see both here and elsewhere, God's love and our love for one another cannot be separated. While God's love is real and God's initiative is prior to our own, we have no warrant to speak about God's love unless we ourselves enact that love in deed and truth (3:18). We must do more than talk about it!

Perhaps a good strategy in preaching from this text would be to pick it up at the end, at the gripping and graphic denial that Christians can love the invisible God if they do not love their own highly visible brothers or sisters (v. 20). John has a gift for stating first principles briefly but in a memorable way, and this is a prime example. One may then move backward, so to speak, to verse 18, where God's love for us, the basis for Christian existence, is succinctly set forth, and forward to verse 21, which grounds mutual love in the command of Jesus. Verses 13–16a may then be viewed as an elaboration upon the fundamental truth of verse 19: "He first loved us"; while verses 16b–18, introducing the themes of the perfection of love and confidence before the day of judgment, deal with the relationship of fear to love. Having introduced the theme of judgment, John must address the possibility of fear. Inasmuch as one of his overarching purposes is to reassure the reader, he wants to stress the absence of fear for the one who is perfected, or fulfilled, in love. This emphasis on the positive side of judgment is entirely consistent with the nature of the gospel itself: It is good news, not bad.

1 John 5:1–5
Love of God Is Keeping His Commandments: Overcoming the World

We have learned already that the proof of loving God is loving his children. Now the obverse is stated: Proof of loving the children of God is loving God and obeying his commandments (5:2). That John takes the love commandment to be directed to, and to apply within, the congregation of believers is again made quite explicit (5:1–2). A logic of love derived from human relationships is invoked to show that loving the believer, who is a child of God, will be the natural reaction of anyone who loves God (5:1) and, of course, believes that Jesus is the Christ, the Son of God (5:5).

The RSV gives a legitimate but less than literal translation of 5:1. The Greek emphasizes the motif of birth: "Everyone who believes that Jesus is the Christ is born of God, and everyone who loves the one who has begotten loves the one begotten of him." Interestingly, the NRSV comes back to a more literal translation: "Everyone who believes that Jesus is the Christ has been born of God." The motif of birth from God, or from above,

117

is quite important in the Gospel and the First Epistle of John (John 1:12–13; 3:3–8; cf. 1 John 3:9) and is continued toward the end of this paragraph. The person born of God overcomes the world (v. 4). As in 1 John 3:9–10 and John 1:12–13, being born (or begotten) of God is explicitly related to being children of God. Birth, or rebirth, from God is a graphic, down-to-earth way of making clear the Christian's participation in the new reality, the new being that God is creating through his Son (2 Cor. 5:17). Such participation is more than a matter of giving intellectual assent or even moral obedience.

The commandments of God (v. 3) are scarcely anything other than those of Christ, and the assertion that loving God is keeping his commandments will scarcely surprise anyone who has read this far in the letter (cf. 2:3), although this precise statement is not found previously. Here it appears as an elucidation of what has just been said (v. 2) both about loving God and about keeping his commandments; now they are equated: to love God *is* to keep his commandments. Probably the author has in mind the word of Jesus in John 14:15: "If you love me, you will keep my commandments" (cf. 15:9–19), which he expects the reader to know. That Jesus' commandments are not burdensome or heavy would follow from their character as commandments (or the commandment) to love one another. This believers should do gladly and joyfully as people now born of God.

In the final statements of this paragraph (vv. 4–5) the theme of overcoming or conquering (NRSV) reappears (cf. 2:13–14; 4:4; John 16:33; also Rev. 2:7, 11, 17, 26, passim). The person born of God overcomes the world (cf. 1 John 2:15–17 on the world) essentially through faith in Jesus, the one who has already overcome the world (John 16:33). The believer is in the world as Jesus is in the world (cf. 1 John 4:17). Thus verse 5 simply reiterates and personifies what has just been said (v. 4). The one who overcomes the world is the believer, who believes specifically that Jesus is the Son of God. Again we should ask whether the emphasis is upon the application of the title "Son of God" to Jesus or upon the fact that it is the man Jesus, the historic fleshly figure who is the Son of God. In this case it is difficult to say. The former interpretation would seem obvious except for the earlier emphasis on the humanity of Jesus (4:1–3; cf. 2:22–23; 2 John 7). To take the statement to mean that it is essential to believe that Jesus is the Son of God makes good sense in light

118

of the Gospel and Epistle. At the same time the other connotation is most likely present also. That is, the Son of God is *Jesus,* the one who has come in flesh, who was from the beginning.

In what does this overcoming or conquest of the world consist? Jesus speaks of overcoming the world as he goes to his death (John 16:33; NRSV: "I have conquered the world!"). Similarly, the phrase "the one who conquers" in the Revelation to John seems to refer or allude to the martyrdom, or the prospect of martyrdom, of confessing Christians. In 1 John, however, the connotations of the term are less dire, although the meaning is related. Those who have conquered the world have risen above it so that it no longer taints or influences, much less determines, them. They have successfully fulfilled the injunction of 1 John 2:15: "Do not love the world or the things in the world."

At this point in 1 John one scarcely expects a new teaching. For the most part John reiterates or rings the changes on points he has already made. Already we have learned that love for God (or of God) is perfected in the one who keeps his commandments (2:5) and that love for the world excludes the love of God. In 3:17 the construction used may mean "God's love" or "love for God," as John makes clear that such love cannot exist where concrete deeds of love for one's fellow Christians are absent. Now love for God is extolled and is said to be the basis or proof of genuine human love, that is, love for one's fellows. Such love for God consists in keeping his commandments, and he commands us to love our brothers and sisters. Thus the ring closes, reflecting the beautiful circularity in John's thought: Love of God and love of our brothers and sisters are mutually dependent. Such love among Christians, together with love for God, who first loved us, separates the beloved community or church from the world. Birth from God, which is correlative to belief in his Son (vv. 4–5), begets the Christian into God's new creation, which is taking shape in this world but is not of it. The otherworldliness of John is not some kind of a material spiritualism irrelevant to this world. Instead, it appears precisely in this world as its judgment. Overcoming the world means living (or dying) in it without succumbing to its lure, without being governed by it, without accepting its standards.

119

Preaching from this pericope should not be difficult, despite the seemingly rambling way in which John's thought progresses. The Common Lectionary extends the lesson for the Sixth Sunday in Easter (cycle B) through verse 6. But verse 6 apparently introduces a new progression of thought, presumably about the nature of Jesus and of the testimony to him. The opening reference to believing that Jesus is the Christ (v. 1) forms an inclusion with believing Jesus is the Son of God (v. 5), clearly delimiting this as a distinct unit of thought.

The unifying theme of the passage is love of God, that is, our human love toward God, which is, of course, predicated first of all on the acceptance of his love as it is manifest in Jesus (cf. 4:9). Heretofore, our love for God has been mentioned but not dwelt upon. Now it becomes the object of more intensive scrutiny. This is a good text on which to base a sermon on loving God. Loving God is something most Christians believe they should do, but it is not a subject about which many nowadays have very much to say. The love of God seems to be some sort of superior spiritual state, which few of us can attain. We are more easily able to deal with mundane things and human relationships, with which most of us are more comfortable.

John interprets the love of God in terms of human love. We show love to God as we love our brothers and sisters. There is no valid love of God where such human love is rejected or absent. In that sense human love seems to take precedence over the love of God, in that it is the sine qua non of love of God. Yet love of God is not simply reducible to human love; that is, love of God is not just another way of talking about love between or among people. We love God first of all by accepting and trusting Jesus his Son. In these verses love of God is said to undergird love of others: "Everyone who loves the parent loves the child"; "By this we know that we love the children of God, when we love God and obey his commandments." This does not mean that love for God can exist where human love is absent or denied. Nevertheless, the concept of love of God denotes a central and indispensable dimension or aspect of Christian existence that is as real and basic as love for one another. The gospel cannot be reduced to a kind of benign humanism with a horizontal, but no vertical, dimension. Our love for each other is beautiful, ennobling, but tinged with sadness and ultimately tragic apart from love of God. In love of God our love for one another finds a permanent place. It does not dissipate into nothingness but remains alive, as God is alive, for God is eternal life.

120

1 John 5:6–13
By Water and by Blood:
The True Testimony of Jesus Christ

The principal theme of this section is witness or testimony (the same word in Greek) to Jesus, the Son of God. Unfortunately, verses 6–8 are most obscure in meaning but apparently important. The remainder of the section is less difficult but nevertheless presents some problems. Although RSV takes 5:6–12 to be a paragraph and thus begins a new paragraph with verse 13, in content and function verse 13 seems to belong more with what precedes it than with what follows, as we shall see. In fact, when verse 13 is included with verses 6–12, this section forms an apt conclusion for 1 John as a whole, taking up themes from the letter's prologue as well as from the final chapter (chap. 20) of the original recension of the Fourth Gospel. (John 21 is clearly a kind of appendix to the Gospel, whether composed and added by the author or, as most scholars think, by one of his disciples.)

What follows (vv. 14–21) has no obvious unity but seems to be a series of comments or notes addressed to several problems and issues that the letter raises or seems to leave unanswered. As such, it may have been penned by the original author, although authorship by a secondary editor cannot be excluded. That the Gospel has a similar conclusion (chap. 21) may have been a relevant precedent for the addition of these verses to 1 John. In reality, we know next to nothing about the earliest transmission and editorial history of the New Testament writings. The fact that John, Mark, and even Romans also have "ending problems" may be significant. Mark ends abruptly at 16:8, giving rise to speculation that its original ending was lost or suppressed; Romans 16, which names many Christians known to have been in Ephesus, has come under suspicion of not having been a part of the letter addressed to Rome but of another recension. However that may be, it is quite within the realm of possibility that an author originally brought the First

Epistle of John to a conclusion at 5:13 and that the remainder was added later, whether by him or by one of his followers.

Certainly there were later additions to the Epistle as it was transmitted in the church. For example, some manuscripts add "amen" at the end (5:21) to afford a more fitting conclusion. The most famous addition, however, is the so-called Johannine Comma of 5:7–8. The King James Version reads: *"For there are three that bear record in heaven, the Father, the Word, and the Holy Ghost: and these three are one.* And there are three that bear witness *in earth,* the spirit, and the water, and the blood: and these three agree in one."* The italicized words are found in no ancient Greek manuscripts but entered the textual tradition by insertion into some Latin manuscripts in the third or fourth century at the earliest. The great sixteenth-century humanist and textual scholar Erasmus thought that this longer reading was spurious but agreed to include it in his printed edition of the Greek New Testament if it could be found in a Greek manuscript. Accordingly, a Greek manuscript with the reading was produced (Codex Montfortianus, now at Trinity College, Dublin), very likely transcribed for this purpose. Erasmus included the reading in subsequent editions. In the same century both Luther and Calvin had doubts about it (Brown, 780), but two centuries later John Wesley argued vigorously for it, devoting a disproportionate amount of space to it in his *Explanatory Notes upon the New Testament.*

The later textual history of 1 John thus suggests that there may have been earlier emendations of the text. Certainly the original author would not have hesitated to make them. Conceivably, he used this same letter on different occasions for different audiences, adapting it for each. In that case, some of the exegetical difficulties we have encountered may reflect such a process. There is, however, no way of knowing about such matters, and we are likely to remain in the dark. In any event, our task is to attempt to interpret the text as it has been transmitted to us. This is the form in which it was accepted as authoritative in the church.

This climactic section of the Epistle (5:6–13) has as its subject matter Jesus Christ, the witness to him, and the life that he brings, thus taking up basic themes of the prologue (1:1–4). We noted that the Epistle's prologue would seem opaque or ob-

122

scure if one did not know the prologue of the Gospel of John. Something analogous might be said of this paragraph as well. If we did not know the prologue of this letter, as well as other important matters contained there and in the Gospel, we would scarcely be able to interpret this text. Although its general subject matter is clear enough, exactly what is being said is not immediately obvious.

At the outset we encounter the most difficult problem. What is meant by the assertion that Jesus Christ came by (or with) water and blood, not with water only? Probably the switch in prepositions (from "by" to "with") is not significant. The problem is what is meant by water and blood. What is referred to, or how is it that he comes by water and blood?

A classic answer in the history of exegesis is that "water" refers to Jesus' baptism by John and "blood" to his death. This interpretation appears very early. By the eighteenth century John Wesley could simply assume that it was the correct one. Moreover, such an interpretation makes good sense in the context of this letter. Not by water only but by blood would mean not by his earthly ministry only (inaugurated by his baptism by John) but by his death. As we have seen, 1 John emphasizes more than the Gospel the saving effect of Jesus' death (1:7; 2:2). Not only so, but John insists upon the fleshliness or humanity of Jesus in the face of those who would deny it (4:2–3; 2 John 7). Jesus' real humanity is epitomized in his death. Thus the insistence on blood as well as water would strike a blow against the erroneous doctrine of the opponents.

An alternative interpretation, favored by Calvin, takes both the water and the blood as an allusion to the death of Jesus, specifically to the scene described in John 19:34–35, where at the piercing of Jesus' side both water and blood flow out. Such an interpretation presupposes that the author was familiar with the Gospel of John and expected that his readers would be as well. In all probability such an assumption is warranted. In that case also the reality of the humanity and death of Jesus would again be underscored, the insistence on not water only but water and blood calling attention to them. Yet on this interpretation the differentiation between water and blood, and the insistence on the latter as well as the former, is harder to understand. On the other understanding of the water as referring to John's baptism of Jesus and the blood to his death, the way in

123

which they are put over against each other is immediately intelligible: water (Jesus' epiphany), yes; but not water only; water *and blood* (Jesus' death).

Interestingly, some early Gnostic Christians, who denied the reality of Jesus' humanity and death (i.e., Docetists; Jesus only *seemed* to be human), thought that the Christ, or the divine presence, descended upon Jesus at his baptism by John and departed from him before his crucifixion or death. Possibly John has this specific form of docetic Christology in view. However that may be, John's references to water and blood almost certainly have to do with the death and humanity of Jesus. Such an interpretation explains them quite intelligibly, particularly in view of what we already know of the context of the Johannine letters and the opponents they have in view.

Although the water evokes the baptism of John and the blood the cross, an allusion to John 19:34–35 may still be found. The motif of *witness* stands out both there and in 1 John 5:6–13. In the Gospel account of the efflux of water and blood a mysterious witness is named (v. 35): "He who saw it has borne witness—his testimony is true, and he knows that he tells the truth—that you also may believe." Although in 1 John 5:7 the Spirit is the witness, the same Spirit is said to be the truth, another distinct echo of John 19:35. The witness of John 19:35 is presumably an historical personage, an eyewitness, not the Spirit, but the Spirit frequently appears in the Gospel as the interpreter of Jesus (14:26). (Significantly, in the Gospel of John the Beloved Disciple and the Spirit have similar or parallel functions, mediating the presence of Jesus to the disciples.) The Spirit as witness is joined in verse 8 by the previously mentioned water and blood. As we have noted above, the distinction between earthly and heavenly witnesses is a later insertion into the text.

At first sight, the water and the blood do not seem to work well as witnesses. It is possible, however, that they have sacramental overtones. If we allow at least a secondary allusion to the blood and water from Jesus' side, the case for a sacramental dimension here becomes even stronger. Certainly the water of baptism and the blood of the Eucharist (Jesus' body and blood) may be construed as witnesses to Jesus, witnesses that agree about his saving work. Moreover, they are witnesses closely related to his death. The Spirit is, according to the Gospel, given only after his death, becoming the inspiration of witness and interpretation (John 7:39; 14:26). Baptism in the early church was taken to recapitulate the death and anticipate the resurrection of Jesus (Rom. 6:4–5). Obviously the Lord's Supper was a participation in Jesus' death. The three witnesses not only pointed back to Jesus but to his death, the epitome of his humanity, and the decisive moment of his redemptive work. Thus they agree. When John speaks of the testimony of God (v. 9), he evidently includes the testimony or witness (the Greek stem, *martyr*, is the same in both cases) of Spirit, water, and blood. Yet finally the testimony of God does not consist in them alone but culminates in a testimony or witness internal to the believer (vv. 10–12). The mention of human testimony is not, however, disparaging or negative. Possibly John 19:35 and the witness attested there is in view, a witness with which the author identifies himself (1 John 1:1–4). His witness is received gladly, but there is a greater witness from God that attests the truth of claims made for Jesus as God's Son. On the other hand, if the water of John's baptism is principally in view, as we have maintained, "the testimony of men" (v. 9; NRSV: "human testimony") likely alludes to John's witness (cf. John 1:6–8, 15, and especially 5:33–36).

That the testimony of God may be spiritual and perhaps also liturgical is borne out by what is said in verses 10–12. Obviously, it is internal or must be internalized (v. 10a). The testimony of the Spirit is appropriated by the Christian who confesses, is baptized, and participates in the worship of the church. The person who rejects these means of God's own testimony rejects God, making him a liar. (This graphic way of speaking, influenced by John's dualism, is obviously not to be taken literally as a statement about God.) We notice that the testimony of men (i.e., human beings) is no longer mentioned. If the witness of the Beloved Disciple or of John the Baptist was thus alluded to (v. 9), it is presumably not in dispute. If the opponents had once stood within the Johannine circle, they presumably would have accepted the testimony of both the Beloved Disciple and John. But they do not really accept the testimony of God. Instead, they represent the spirit of error, and they do not rightly receive or interpret the water and the blood—at least in John's view. Their rejection of the water and blood presumably has to do with their denying the humanity and death of Jesus as effecting salvation. Whether they also do not receive the sacra-

125

ments is a question we can no longer answer. At least they have broken communion *(koinōnia)* with the author and stand outside his community.

This discussion of testimony to Jesus recalls John 5:31–39, where the testimony of the Baptist, of Jesus' works, and of the Father are mentioned. One is tempted to pair off the testimony of the Baptist with water, that of Jesus' works with blood, and that of the Father with the Spirit, and thus correlate the two passages. But while John 5:31–39 may hover in the background of our passage, such analogies should not be pressed. The highly allusive character of our text has already been noted, together with the possibility that more than one passage in the Gospel may be in view.

The internal nature of God's testimony is driven home in verse 11. At bottom it is the eternal life that is given in God's Son, Jesus Christ. Spirit, water, and blood are means of access to Jesus Christ, or, to put matters more accurately, they are God's or Christ's means of access to us. Yet salvation as the gift of life through the Son is the ultimate testimony of God. It is an internal, spiritual testimony. To say that it is dependent on no external reality or witness would, however, be inaccurate. The sending of the Son, his ministry and death, are external to us, and John would not doubt that for a moment. Also, such a witness as that of the Baptist, or the Beloved Disciple, would not be disparaged. Nevertheless, the witness of God, which if effective causes the rebirth of the believer into eternal life, is the ultimate assurance, and it is finally internal to the person engaged with the gospel. It is confirmed by the Spirit and is the means by which grace is bestowed within the believer and the church.

The themes of testimony or witness and life in this concluding section of the letter remind us of the prologue (1:1–4). Indeed, they constitute a kind of inclusion with the prologue and indicate the intention of the author to tie basic themes together as he brings his work to a conclusion. The final statements underscore the theme of life, which is central to the Gospel and characteristic of the Johannine literature. John's dualism, which recurs throughout the letter, finds definitive expression in verse 12: Having the Son means life, not having the Son means that one does not have life. Thus the NRSV's "whoever," replacing the RSV's "he who," is particularly appropriate. The members of the Johannine community, with other Christians, have life,

126

provided they are all faithful to the true doctrine of Christ, make the right confession, and obey Christ's commands.

John now reassures his readers that having believed in the Son, their eternal life through and with him is assured. Thus he sums up his purpose in writing (v. 13). He writes to those who believe, and in believing obey, in order that they may know. Knowledge is based on the reality of faithful obedience to God's word in the gospel, that is, in Jesus Christ, his Son. What is said here in this regard recalls, probably intentionally, the concluding colophon of the first recension of the Fourth Gospel (20:31). There John says that "these [signs] are written that you may believe that Jesus is the Christ, the Son of God, and that believing you may have life in his name." Although the concluding statements differ in emphasis, belief in the name of Jesus Christ as the Son of God to the end that the believer might have eternal life is the burden of both. Possibly both the Gospel and Epistle once ended with such eloquent statements, but neither seems to have been published without the present conclusions, which are attested in all existing manuscripts.

Our struggle to understand this text already indicates that no clear, fresh Christian teaching leaps out from it. Yet there are here, as we have seen, important issues that have to do with Christology and the sacraments. The introduction of the three heavenly witnesses in verse 8, KJV, although plainly a secondary reading, betokens the importance of this text in theological discussions through the centuries. Further reflection is called for and will prove worthwhile.

That Jesus Christ came by water and blood seems at first to be a rather obscure and not very profitable statement. Yet when examined closely in relation to the letter's christological teaching, it turns out to be the author's way of emphasizing the humanity of Jesus, and particularly the saving effect of his death. Thus John underscores the right and true confession of Jesus' coming in the flesh, presumably against the separatist opponents who do not acknowledge it. While 1 John 5:6–8 would be quite obscure if isolated and taken out of context, when seen in the context and setting of the Johannine letters, the meaning is not hard to fathom. The character and importance of the christological controversy observed earlier in the letter is confirmed.

127

Moreover, the role of Spirit, water, and blood as witnesses

is intriguing. The role of the Spirit as witness is not difficult to conceive. If we are correct in seeing in the witnessing function of water and blood an allusion to the sacraments of baptism and the Lord's Supper, another dimension is added, and we get some sense of the worship life of the Johannine churches. The Evangelist strongly insists upon devouring Jesus' flesh and blood, presumably in the Eucharist, as a necessity for anyone who desires participation in him (John 6:52–58). Probably his insistence had in view Jews or Jewish Christians who still lived and worshiped within the synagogue. Here in the Epistle John directs his words to loyal followers, but he may also have in view Christians who ignore the Eucharist or somehow do not practice or understand it properly. Ignatius, the early second-century bishop of Antioch, knew about such Christians; it is possible John has them in mind, but we cannot say more.

The Spirit, water, and blood taken together effect, or participate in, the witness or testimony of God (v. 9), which is said to be greater than the witness of human beings. As we noted, the latter is probably not just human testimony generally but contains an allusion to John the Baptist, if not to the testimony or witness to Jesus referred to in 1:1–4 and at a number of points in the Gospel of John. For John human witness, in the sense of those who have seen and heard, is essential to the propagation of the Gospel. Yet it avails nothing without the internal testimony of the Holy Spirit and the worship and sacraments of the church. (In this connection we should note that our use of "sacrament" is somewhat anachronistic, for no such generic term is used in the New Testament of baptism and the Lord's Supper.) That the testimony of God is finally eternal life (v. 11) means that it is indeed internal, but this does not contradict its relationship to the three witnesses of Spirit, water, and blood mentioned earlier. These witnesses are means by which eternal life is planted in the human spirit.

Preaching from this text will require interpretation, and some such explanation as we have given will necessarily be part of the sermon. Otherwise, the text remains opaque. The Common Lectionary reading for the Seventh Sunday in Easter (cycle B) is 5:9–13. By omitting 5:6–8, the problem of the meaning of the water and blood, as well as their function as witnesses, is avoided. But apart from them it is impossible to explain adequately the meaning of the witness or testimony of God (vv. 9–11). Therefore, one must begin with verse 6.

Obviously, a sermon on this text will be exegetical and doctrinal. Since a good part of it will involve explaining the text, that means explaining the doctrine, whether christological, sacramental, or soteriological. Indeed, all three. The experiential element, that is, the testimony of eternal life, is essential and important but cannot be separated from the christological and the sacramental, nor indeed from the historical, for we have seen that the "testimony of men" (v. 9) probably includes the valid eyewitnesses that the Gospel and Epistle also represent.

It would be tempting to begin at the end (vv. 11–13) and work backward in explaining this text, as we, in fact, suggested in the case of 4:13–21. This is not an impossible procedure here and may be a good homiletical tactic as long as one keeps in view the christological, sacramental, and traditional (eyewitness) grounds of the proclamation of life that are indispensable to the claim to possess it. Eternal life is a possession, but first of all a gift. By tying the claim to possess life to the elements of witness or testimony emphasized earlier in the pericope, one also avoids the danger of extolling something as a possession that many of the congregation may not be consciously experiencing. Eternal life is the outcome of a specific testimony, not a general religious feeling or state of consciousness. It is all too easy, and theologically erroneous, to identify eternal life with such a religious feeling or psychological state, which may or may not be related to the revelation of God in Jesus Christ. John speaks of eternal life not as a psychological experience of "uplift" but as a reality given by God. He is not saying, "Experience eternal life so that you may have it," but rather, "You have eternal life; know this in order that you may experience it." The author writes to reassure his readers or hearers, as the preacher should reassure the congregation on the basis of this word.

REFLECTION:
The Opponents of John

The difficulty of interpreting 1 John 5:6–8, and particularly the references to water and blood, highlights the problem of understanding the Johannine letters generally. Obviously 1 John, and the shorter letters as well, address a situation of controversy and deal with the views and activities of opponents. As we observed in the introduction, however, we are privileged to hear only one side of the discussion or debate in progress. We do not know exactly what the addressees had thought or said, much less what opponents or separatists, whom the author calls antichrists, actually believed. Indeed, it is not always clear what views the author imputes to them. In regard to such opponents, at least two major questions have occupied scholarship. First, does the author of the letters fight on one front or several? That is, are the opponents united? Are the erroneous christological views that he rejects and the ethical failings that he condemns to be ascribed to the same party or group? Second, what exactly was the heretical christological view that he rejected? Was the author attacking a full-blown gnostic or docetic heresy, according to which the humanity of Jesus was set aside or denied?

We have not undertaken to treat either of these questions comprehensively in the exegesis of this commentary, although we have made clear that the author was faced with opposition from within the Christian community and in all probability from people who had been closely associated with him at one time. Moreover, a substantial aspect of this opposition was a clearly inadequate and erroneous christological teaching that at least some of the opponents were promulgating widely.

In his magisterial commentary, Raymond Brown has defended the thesis that the author basically fought on only one front: The errors and sins he denounces were perceived by him as the hallmarks of a common group of opponents (see Brown, *The Epistles of John*, pp. 49–68, esp. pp. 49–50). Moreover— and this is the more original aspect of Brown's thesis—the adversaries were closely related to the author himself. They were also "Johannine Christians" in that they referred to the Gospel

130

of John and the Johannine traditions as the basis for their authority and teaching. The author and his opponents were, in
effect, fighting over the proper understanding of Johannine
theology, indeed, the correct interpretation of the Gospel of
John (Brown, pp. 69–115). The opponents pushed the teaching
of the Gospel of John in wrong directions. They exaggerated the
uniqueness or divinity of Jesus to the detriment, a setting aside,
of his humanity. Yet in doing so they were in touch with a
genuine aspect of the Fourth Gospel, which sets forth Jesus'
divinity like no other Gospel. By the same token, the opponents
laid claim to the promises of Jesus, who in the Fourth Gospel
pronounces his disciples already beyond judgment and death,
in the present, the here and now. Not unreasonably they understood themselves to be free from sin. Students interested in
pursuing this question, and the entire set of problems having to
do with the historical setting and purpose of the Johannine
letters, should begin by consulting Brown. Whether John con-
fronts only one set of opponents can probably never be determined with certainty, but the hypothesis of their unity works
well in that it allows us to make good sense of the various texts.

As to the nature of the opponents' Christology, there is at
least a predominant point of view, if not a complete consensus.
We have taken the position in the commentary that the opponents denied the humanity of Jesus Christ. More precisely, they
denied the revelatory and salvific significance of the human
Jesus. At least John attributes such a position to them. This
attribution is clearest in 1 John 4:2–3 and 2 John 7, and makes
intelligible what is said about water and blood in 5:6–8. Moreover, the prologue's emphasis on the visibility, audibility, and
tangibility of Jesus at the very outset of 1 John fits this picture
well. Whether the accusation against the opponents is justified
is again impossible to say, unless one assumes that the canonical
writer must be accurate and correct. On the other hand, that
John thinks his accusation is justified would seem a safe assumption. But there is also another consideration.

The denial of the humanity of Jesus Christ was a staple of
some second-century Christologies that were eventually condemned as heretical. Such a denial, commonly associated with
Gnosticism, is called "docetic" from the Greek verb *dokein*,
meaning "to seem." Christ only seemed to be human but in
reality was not. The divine Christ might even be separated from
the human Jesus. If the opponents of 1 John espoused such a

131

view, they would be the first Docetists of whom we have any knowledge. Brown, who takes the author's stricture seriously as pointing to a deficient Christology of this sort, is nevertheless reluctant to hang the docetic label on John's opponents or to maintain that they represented what might be called a full-blown docetic Christology. Nor does he find sufficient evidence to identify them with any ancient heretic, such as Cerinthus, or with any specific group mentioned by early Christian heresiologists. The majority of commentators are, if anything, less cautious than Brown. Martin Luther mentions Cerinthus, the Jews, and the pope among those who deny that Jesus actually came in the flesh. Among modern scholars, such commentators as Brooke and Houlden in Great Britain, and Bultmann, Schnackenburg, and most recently, Strecker in Germany have taken something like the position we have espoused. As we have pointed out, John is clearly countering a Christian interpretation or Christology that he opposes. Not confessing Jesus can therefore scarcely mean that the opponents are simply not, or do not claim to be, Christians. The opponents hold views about Jesus that John regards as deplorable. If their Christology is not, as it seems, docetic, we can scarcely say much about it.

1 John 5:14–21
Epilogue: This Is the Confidence We Have in Him: On What to Pray For

If one sees in 5:13 the conclusion of the letter, which reiterates motifs from the original conclusion of the Gospel (20:31), 5:14–21 must appear to be a kind of postscript. On first reading, we find that several matters are dealt with. The most important point made by the author (or possibly by a later editor), however, and apparently the reason for the postscript, is his encouragement to the readers to pray for sinners who have not committed a mortal sin ("unto death"; vv. 16–17). The rest of the paragraph leads up to and away from this instruction.

The subject of prayer is broached in a rather general way (v. 14) and is reminiscent of what is said by Jesus in the Gospels. His saying about asking and receiving (Matt. 7:7) is paralleled by several similar assurances in the Gospel of John (14:13; 15:7; 16:23). Apparently, our author reiterates this teaching in view of a qualification he must now make. Such a blanket assurance by Jesus of the fulfillment of petitions in prayer has, through the succeeding centuries, doubtless puzzled a great many Christians whose prayers have not been answered in the way they would have hoped. In verse 15 John may actually speak to that issue. Interestingly enough, John does not promise that "we shall obtain" what we ask but states flatly that "we have [RSV and NRSV: "have obtained"] the requests made of him." It is as if he is telling his readers that Jesus' promise assures them that what they have gotten is what they asked for, that is, the answer to their prayer petition. This may seem at first a somewhat circular argument. Jesus promised to fulfill your petitions. You petitioned in prayer. Therefore, what you have received is by definition the answer to your prayer. Of course, what they have received is eternal life (v. 13). Need they ask for anything more? In fact, this general statement about prayer, traditional in origin, looks ahead to the question of what brother or sister one ought to pray for.

Accordingly, John discusses prayer for fellow Christians who have sinned against the background of Jesus' assurance of answered prayer. The initial statement (v. 16a) anticipates that the Christian will pray for the brother or sister committing a sin that is "not a mortal sin" (literally, "not a sin unto death") and that by his prayer he will give that sinner life. The RSV (followed by NRSV) substitutes "God" for "he" ("God will give him life"), and this makes good sense theologically, although the obvious antecedent of the pronoun is the one offering prayer. Thus the Greek clause is most naturally translated: "He will ask, and he will give him life for those whose sin is not unto death." The literal translation emphasizes even more strongly the importance of the role of the one who prays for the sinner. Having encouraged prayer for sin that is not mortal, John next discourages prayer for sin that is mortal, or unto death (v. 16b). Apparently, John intends to forbid prayer for such a one, although he does not put it in quite those terms. Perhaps in view of Jesus' comprehensive invitation to pray, he cannot forbid such prayer, but he certainly can and does discourage it.

What is mortal sin or the sin unto death? Not surprisingly, John's distinction between sin that is mortal and sin that is not has launched an avalanche of exegetical and theological discus-

sion. The subject holds an endless fascination for religious people and has a rich background, and foreground, in the Old
Testament and ancient Judaism, as well as early and medieval
Christianity. One thinks immediately of the distinction between unintentional and intentional sin in the Old Testament
(cf. Lev. 4; Num. 15:27–31; Deut. 17:12). The New Testament
also offers ample evidence for a distinction in seriousness among
sins and sinners. In Mark 3:29 par. Jesus refers to an unforgiv-
able blasphemy against the Holy Spirit, and Christians ever
since have speculated what that might be in order to avoid it.
Paul recommends the ostracism or excommunication, if not the
death, of the unrepentant perpetrator of a heinous sin (1 Cor.
5:5). Hebrews speaks more than once of Christians who have
apostasized or sinned deliberately (6:4–8; 10:26–31) and for
whom there is no further hope of restoration or repentance.
Obviously the early church had to deal with the problem of sin
after conversion and baptism, something that should not exist
but did. The postapostolic *Shepherd of Hermas,* one of the early
writings known as the Apostolic Fathers, treats the question at
great length. Doubtless this statement in 1 John is to be seen
against this background.

Later on the church would distinguish between mortal sins
(pride, covetousness, lust, envy, gluttony, anger, and sloth) and
venial sins, but as far as we know, this is a much later distinction.
In somewhat the same vein, Tertullian identified the sins unto
death of which John speaks as murder, idolatry, injustice, apostasy, adultery, and fornication (Brown, p. 616). Not a bad list!
There is, of course, no way of determining whether these sins
are what John had in mind. In fact, we cannot be entirely sure
that Tertullian's instinct that John was referring to more heinous sins, while entirely reasonable, is correct. Perhaps "sin
unto death" and "sin not unto death" have more to do with the
status and place of the sinner than with the sin itself.

Mortal sin may be unconfessed sin, sin of which the sinner
has not repented. Such sin, if not confessed publicly, is mortal
in the sense that it leads to death. Yet John has promised· "If we
confess our sins, he is faithful and just, and will forgive our sins
and cleanse us from all unrighteousness" (1:9). Thus those who
have confessed are forgiven and cleansed. Nothing stands in the
134   way of praying for them. This seems an attractive proposal, but
if they have confessed their sin, why does one still need to pray
for them? Moreover, the way the subject is introduced, "If any

one sees his brother committing what is not a mortal sin . . ."
seems to indicate that the sin is not yet confessed. One sees the
brother or sister doing it; a space of time in which confession
and forgiveness would be possible is not contemplated. We
seem therefore to be back to the problem of what kind of sin.

Yet the question of the identity of the sinners may not be
entirely misplaced. Throughout the letter John has inveighed
against the separatists, opponents, and antichrists. They have
broken the unity of the community (2:18–19) and have departed from the true confession that the human Jesus is the Son
of God (4:2–3). Are they in mind when John specifically excludes
prayer for mortal sin, and presumably for the ones who have
sinned mortally? Perhaps it is significant that John envisions
seeing a brother or sister who has committed a sin that is not
mortal, but does not speak of actually seeing a *brother* or *sister*
commit a mortal sin. That is, the person committing such a sin
is not described as a brother or sister. The possibility of mortal
sin appears, so to speak, at the periphery of his vision.

Quite conceivably those who have committed the sin unto
death are the Johannine Christians who have separated themselves and now lie beyond the pale. They have thus become
guilty of mortal sin as they have willfully rejected John's admo-
nitions and have chosen to put themselves beyond his community *(koinōnia)* and jurisdiction, not confessing that Jesus Christ
has come in the flesh. Without doubt, in John's view those who
have followed the opponents have followed them into darkness
and death. Therefore, their sin would be, quite literally, "unto
death." All sin is wrongdoing, just as sin is iniquity (3:4), but
there is a sin that is not mortal (5:17). Note that John does not
say, "some forms of wrongdoing are worse than others," but
instead reaffirms the fact that not all sin leads to death. Would
he agree that sins kept within the community, confessed and
forgiven there, do not lead to death, but sin outside the community, or the sin of breaking the community, does, in fact, lead
to death? It is tempting to think this is the distinction he has in
mind, but the evidence stops short of proof. Interestingly
enough, Martin Luther, in his lectures on 1 John, says that
mortal sins "are those of the heretics, who are hardened after
one or another rebuke. . . . For other sins . . . I can pray that they
be remitted and not imputed. For heretics I cannot do this
when they do not acknowledge their sin." John Wesley identified the sin unto death as total apostasy.

135

The distinction just made leads the author to reiterate what he has said earlier about the sinlessness of Christians (5:18; cf. 3:9). But what can he mean in view of the statement about sins that are not mortal that he has just made? That statement indicates quite plainly that such sins are committed by Christians. The present tenses in verse 18 help us, for the sentence can quite legitimately be rendered as follows: "We know that everyone who is born of God does not continue in sin, but the one who was begotten [or born] of God [i.e., Jesus] is keeping him, and the evil one is not touching him." We have translated all the present tenses with their full, continuative sense so as to emphasize the present state of born-again Christians without creating the impression that freedom from sin is a kind of automatic process that removes them from the realm of any meaningful moral decision. Such a reading of this text agrees not only with 1:8, 10; 2:1–2, but with what has been said just previously. Martin Luther summed it up quite well: "At times a person is overtaken [by sin] when that birth is not sustained on the basis of the Word of God and the flesh prevails, so that he does what he would not do in other circumstances. At times the Spirit overcomes unbelief and emotions, and thus he does not sin." The one who is born or begotten of God (v. 18) is pretty clearly Jesus himself; the original text scarcely permits any other construction. Although Jesus is not spoken of in precisely this way earlier on in the letter, he twice is called "only begotten" (RSV and NRSV translate "only") in the Gospel of John (1:18; 3:16), in both cases in close proximity to references to Christians being born of God. The evil one who is not touching the Christian is, of course, Satan.

The next statement (v. 19) seems almost gratuitous, but it is actually occasioned by what has just been written. The knowledge that the readers are of God in effect equates them with those born of God (v. 18), a thoroughly Johannine thought. The NRSV freely, but aptly, translates: "We know that we are God's children." Otherwise, the world is in the power of Satan. The mentioning of the world at this point confirms our suggestion that the opponents, who are of the world (4:5), are in view in verse 16b. The contrast between God and the Satan-dominated world reflects the dualism we have seen so often in 1 John.

136

This dualistic contrast is implied in the final affirmation of the knowledge and status of Christians (v. 20). They belong to the truth, to God and Christ. Again, the motif of reassurance is prominent: "And we know. . . ." The letter concludes with one of the relatively few New Testament affirmations that Jesus is God, which is strikingly reminiscent of the concluding word of Thomas in the Gospel (20:28): "My Lord and my God!" Also, the identification of Jesus with eternal life recalls the letter's prologue, where Jesus is called the "word of life" (1:1) and "the eternal life which was with the Father and was made manifest to us" (1:2). Even if verses 14–21 were added later, this conclusion, by picking up motifs from the beginning, forms an inclusion and thus again is an appropriate ending for the letter.

The last word (v. 21) is brief and puzzling. Nothing in the letter prepares us for the final warning about idols except the fact that in the previous summation Jesus is called not only "God" but the true God, implying that there are false gods, i.e., idols. Now the Christian is warned away from them. The address "little children" is quite typical of John. The question is, of course, what is meant by idols. That John has in mind actual idolatry—still amply represented in the ancient world (1 Thess. 1:9; Acts 17:23)—is unlikely since until this point the object of his polemic has been internal, intrachurchly opposition. There has been no mention of pagan religion. Probably "idolatry" is to be understood with reference to opponents, whose false Christology, false understanding of Jesus, is taken to be idolatrous. By way of contrast, John's followers adhere to the right and proper confession of Jesus Christ, the *true* God, who means eternal life for those who believe.

Any teaching and preaching values in this text require careful delineation, but they are nevertheless present. The problem that we have had in defining sins that are mortal and sins that are not should not prevent us from seeing the importance of such a text as this in the development of ways of dealing with postbaptismal sin in the early church. In the first flush of enthusiasm postbaptismal sin may not have loomed so large, although already for Paul it was a shocking contradiction of the new life in Christ (Rom. 6:1–4). As time passed a new generation came on the scene, however; further sin was increasingly recognized as a serious and continuing problem that needed to be attended to by the establishment of church discipline and rules of penance. We may suspect that John's distinction between sins that are mortal and those that are not has something to do with the intrachurch conflict in which he was engaged. The distinction

137

that he makes became important in Christian thinking on the subject. As a text for teaching or preaching, 1 John 5:14–21 could become the basis for a discussion about the necessity of discipline and repentance, not only individually but as corporate or public acts. While Protestants have for centuries been fond of attacking the Catholic form of penance, penance itself has become a lost discipline in non-Catholic churches.

One of John's recurring statements to the effect that Christians do not sin appears here at the end (5:18). We have already noticed the tension between such statements (cf. 3:6, 9–10) and exhortations to repent in view of the fact that no one is free of sin (1:8; 1:10—2:2). The contradiction is so blatant that the author could scarcely have been unaware of it. We have cited Luther's sane balancing of the issue, which goes beyond what John actually says but probably points us in the right direction. Also John Calvin writes: "If you imagine God's children to be completely pure and free from sin, as the fanatics contend, the apostle is inconsistent, for he would be taking away the mutual duty of prayer among brethren" (which he just set out in v. 16). The tension in John's thought seems to have its basis in a state of affairs that, while contradictory, nevertheless continues to exist for Christians in the world. Insofar as they are born of God and participate in the new reality he is bringing about, they do not sin. But, in fact, nobody's participation *(koinōnia)* is complete or perfect, and this reality must be recognized and dealt with. In Christ and in the community the resources for dealing with it are available. While John cannot concede to sin any jurisdiction over Christians whatsoever, at the same time he cannot and does not refuse to grant the reality of sin. It will not go away because it is denied but only if Christ deals with it as, of course, he has and will.

THE BOOK OF
Second John

2 John 1–3
The Elder and the Elect Lady: Anonymous Figures of the Ancient Church

The identity of the Elder is unknown (see Introduction). By tradition he is John, the son of Zebedee, but if that were the case, it seems odd that he should refer to himself as an elder rather than an apostle (contrast the salutation in many of Paul's letters). Actually, there was an Elder John in the ancient church, whom Papias (early second century) and Eusebius (early fourth century) distinguish from the Apostle John. At least Eusebius, quoting Papias (*EH* 3.39.3–4), understands him to refer to two different persons, and most modern scholars agree with the distinction. Yet even granted the existence of such an Elder John, there is no evidence that he was the author of this letter beyond the fact that it is attributed to John by church tradition. Both 2 and 3 John purport to come from the Elder, who in customary ancient epistolary fashion names himself with the recipient at the beginning of the letter (cf. again Paul's letters). Second John is unique in the New Testament in using a title rather than the proper name of the addressee.

The identity of the addressee, the Elect Lady *(eklektē kyria)* and her children, is also a question. Is she a person or does the author thus personify the church to whom he is writing? Probably the latter, although this has not been universally accepted and *eklektē* has even been taken as a form of a proper name ("Electa"). But the reference to an elect sister and her children in verse 13 virtually eliminates the possibility that we have here a proper name, while supporting the view that "Elect Lady" is a way of referring to a church, a specific Christian congregation.

Readers may wonder why 2 and 3 John possess the standard

139

epistolary form of address and conclusion while 1 John does not. Because of this, although 2 and 3 John are attributed to the Elder, 1 John, having no salutation, is attributed to no one. Theories of multiple authorship abound, but we take the simplest, and traditional, position that such theories are not necessary to explain the letters. Possibly 1 John was a general communication, intended for reading in several of the Johannine communities or churches. Thus it lacks a specific epistolary address, as well as a conclusion. On the other hand, 2 and 3 John are clearly addressed to specific congregations and convey messages appropriate to each. Without doubt 3 John presupposes a distinct set of circumstances to which the Elder addresses himself. This seems to be somewhat less the case with 2 John, which in content at least is much more closely related to 1 John. In fact, it consists of a reiteration of one or two aspects of the message of 1 John but with related instructions that presuppose a quite specific situation.

The greeting (vv. 1–2) is cast in typical Johannine language: love, truth, knowledge, abiding. We know the concepts well from 1 John, as well as from the Gospel. That the Elder loves the Christians to whom he writes is not at all surprising. The author, referring back to Jesus' command (cf. v. 5), frequently urges love for one another. Yet only here and in 3 John does he express directly his own love for those to whom he writes. At the same time he joins his love to that of others. "Truth" for the Johannine community is a christological term, or one loaded with christological implications (cf. John 14:6). "In the truth" here is the Johannine equivalent of Paul's "in Christ." "All who know the truth" really means all who know the truth of God that is incarnate in Jesus Christ, as the following clause (v. 2) shows. What is said of the truth here applies exactly to Jesus Christ.

The opening benediction (v. 3), in some contrast to the preceding Johannine salutation, sounds quite Pauline. Every Pauline letter except Galatians contains such a benediction or blessing at the conclusion of the salutation. That grace, mercy, and peace are traditionally Pauline is evident not least from the Pauline Pastorals, where they twice occur in exactly this combination and order (1 Tim. 1:2; 2 Tim. 1:2). Paul himself says "Grace to you and peace" fairly consistently, however. 1 Peter has "grace and peace," as do 2 Peter and even Revelation (1:4). One could scarcely argue that we have here a conscious imita-

140

tion of Paul, any more than in 1 or 2 Peter (or in Jude for that matter), but John's usage may indicate how much Paul influenced early Christian epistolary style generally.

"Grace" *(charis)* is a typically Pauline theological term, which occurs but four other times in the Johannine writings, all in the prologue of the Gospel. "Peace" *(eirēnē)* occurs in John only on the lips of Jesus in the farewell discourses and resurrection scenes. "Mercy" *(eleos)* is found only here in the Johannine writings. The famous Aaronic benediction of Numbers 6:24–26 in the LXX combines the concepts of mercy and peace, although RSV translates "be merciful" as "be gracious," which, incidentally, shows how the two concepts overlap in biblical thought. The concluding "in truth and love" (2 John 3) adds a distinctly Johannine ring to the otherwise traditional benediction.

While the salutation contains no distinctive teaching, it is not unimportant as an indication of the character and interests of Johannine Christianity and early Christianity generally. There underlies this letter, and specifically this greeting, an assumption, indeed, a conviction, about the unity of the church. That the unity is assumed rather than debated is not in itself insignificant. Love and knowledge of the truth bind the community together.

The Elder writes to a church for which he evidently feels responsible, both for the conduct of its members (vv. 4–6) and their doctrine (vv. 7–11). We have noticed that unlike Paul he does not style himself an apostle. This may seem curious, inasmuch as the authority he presumes to exercise would seem very much like Paul's apostolic authority (cf. esp. v. 12). Perhaps the Elder represents a form of early Christianity in which apostolic or similar office played little role. Yet the fact that he finds it necessary to exercise what amounts to apostolic authority to underscore Jesus' own teaching and the right doctrine about him gives one pause in claiming this. Even if he rejected apostolic authority and church office, the very role he filled demonstrated their necessity in the church! This quasiapostolic function is in the service of the gospel, of course, and the necessary corollary or counterpoise of the gospel is the church. One gospel, one church. The Elder does not make this equation, but it is scarcely conceivable that he could countenance many different gospels with correspondingly different and separate churches. Indeed, both the Gospel (17:21, 23) and the First Epistle (1:3–4; 2:19) underscore the importance of unity. What

141

is said in the name of Paul in Ephesians (4:4–6) would have been subscribed to gladly by our Elder: "There is one body and one Spirit, just as you were called to the one hope that belongs to your call, one Lord, one faith, one baptism, one God and Father of us all, who is above all and through all and in all." Paul himself probably did not live to see it and say it in quite that way, but Ephesians gives us a legitimate extension and interpretation of Paul's meaning with which the author of the Johannine literature would have doubtless agreed.

2 John 4–11
Following the Truth:
Right Conduct and Confession

Some, but presumably not all, members of the church to which John writes are following the truth, or, as the NRSV accurately translates, walking in the truth (v. 4). Because only some are walking in the truth, however, the danger represented by the opponents and secessionists is very real indeed. Our author will later dwell on this danger (vv. 7–11). The idea of being commanded by the Father is not unusual. Jesus has received his commandment from the Father (John 10:18), and although we think of the disciples as normally receiving their orders from Jesus (2:7–11; 3:11), John can and does speak of obeying God's commandments (e.g., 3:22–24; 5:2–3).

Not surprisingly, however, the Elder next refers to the love commandment of Jesus (John 13:34; cf. 1 John 2:7–11; 3:11–18), and exactly as in 1 John plays upon the difference between new and old, "the one we have had from the beginning" (v. 5). Again he addresses the Lady *(kyria),* using the feminine form of the title so often applied to Jesus in the New Testament, *kyrios,* Lord. (It is not very likely that the feminine form of *kyrios,* any more than the masculine, would be applied to another person age by a Christian in the New Testament; hence he is probably referring to a church.)

142   The RSV translation gets the sense of verse 6, but the NRSV's literal rendering is more graphic: "And this is love, that we walk according to his commandments; this is the commandment just

as you have heard it from the beginning—you must walk in it." Apparently with verse 5 and the reference to a new commandment, the antecedent of "his" ("his commandments") in verse 6 becomes Jesus instead of God. As we have noted, however, whether the Father or the Son commands makes little difference; they have the same authority. The shift from the plural "commandments" to the singular is familiar and typical. The commandments can be reduced to the single commandment to walk in love.

The biblical imagery of walking for conducting one's life is familiar enough still. To walk in love is to walk in Jesus' own way, to use John's imagery, to walk as he walked (1 John 2:6). So walking in the truth (v. 4) is walking in Jesus' commandments (v. 6) or walking as he walked. The metaphor of walking is deeply rooted in the Bible and in ancient Jewish tradition: "O house of Jacob, come, let us walk in the light of the Lord" (Isa. 2:5); "Come, let us go up to the mountain of the Lord . . . that he may teach us his ways and that we may walk in his paths" (Isa. 2:3; cf. Micah 4:2). In Proverbs, Wisdom says: "I walk in the way of righteousness, in the paths of justice" (8:20). The Pharisees and scribes ask Jesus, "Why do your disciples not walk according to the tradition of the elders?" (Mark 7:5). The technical Hebrew term for legal admonition based on law is *halakah* (walking). Paul speaks of walking according to love (Rom. 14:15), and so forth. The imagery of walking is ancient but still meaningful.

In verses 7–11 the letter takes a turn in a new direction, as the paragraph division of the NRSV indicates. The "for" (or "because" of v. 7) should, following conventional rules of syntax, refer to the immediately preceding statement. In terms of the total sense of the paragraph, however, it would seem to refer ultimately to verse 4, where John speaks of his exceeding joy that some of the children of the Elect Lady are walking in truth, "for many deceivers have gone out into the world." The NRSV drops "for," despite the fact that it is found in the Greek text *(gar),* perhaps because this more remote connection is not recognized. One cannot, however, divorce this causal statement (v. 7a) from the immediately preceding exhortation to love. The opponents do not walk in love, and thus they show the darkness of their way (cf. 1 John 2:9–11; 3:15; 4:20). Living and walking in love is walking in the truth; certainly this is not separable from making the proper confession of Jesus Christ, who came

143

and died in the flesh, thus expressing his love for us (1 John 3:16; John 15:12–13). To walk in love is to guard the truth and to guard against the deceivers.

The deceivers' going out into the world signals their breaking of community (1 John 1:3; 2:18–19) and their departure from the truth (4:1–5). They espouse a docetic Christology that denies the fleshliness of Jesus Christ. Thus they show themselves to be deceivers and antichrists (cf. 1 John 2:18, 26; 3:7; 4:3). Obviously, we have here evidence of the existence of the same opponents and false teaching we encountered in 1 John. In fact, only here is their false confession, that is, their failure to confess "that Jesus Christ has come *in the flesh*" (NRSV), made entirely explicit. Although the false teachers and their heresy are now briefly described, we have the impression that this is not the first time the readers have heard of them. That is, the way they are mentioned is what we would expect if they were already known to the intended readers from 1 John. They are identified, and John quickly moves ahead to describe the danger they represent to the community and specifically to the readers.

Apparently, the danger is contamination by association, and the way to avoid contamination is to have nothing to do with such people (cf. vv. 10–11). One is reminded of the warnings of the Pauline Pastorals (1 Tim. 6:20–21; 2 Tim. 2:14–19, 23; Titus 3:9–11). John is not above appealing to his readers' self-interests, as he urges them, in effect, not to squander their good standing (v. 8). The concept of reward to obedient Christians is not unique to John. Paul certainly shared it (1 Cor. 3:14–15), as did most early Christians (cf. Matt. 25:31–46).

Presumably the people who are described as going ahead and not abiding (v. 9) are the same as the heretics of verse 7. (The NRSV takes some liberty with the Greek by speaking of going beyond the teaching of Christ, but that is apparently what is meant.) If so, the reader knows their distinctive, and offensive, christological doctrine, so there is no need to reiterate it. It is important to observe that these false teachers are described as innovators. This is what their "going ahead" and not abiding in the doctrine of Christ appears to mean. Such a meaning corresponds with the perspective of 1 John as it has appeared from 1:1–4 onward. The true doctrine, like the love commandment, is what the followers of Jesus and the Elder have had from

144

the beginning. What is old is true, particularly if it goes back to Jesus.

The doctrine (RSV) or teaching (NRSV) of Christ in which all are to abide is apparently the doctrine about Christ and not what Jesus himself taught; thus the RSV's rendering is preferable. The Greek word used, *didachē,* can mean teaching in the sense of moral instruction (Rom. 6:17), but it does not seem to have that meaning here. The word is in fact used of the teaching of Jesus in the Fourth Gospel (John 7:16–17; 18:19), but there it seems to mean principally his christological teaching, which is the doctrine about him. Interestingly enough, the term "to abide" *(menein),* previously used of abiding in Jesus and in God (e.g., 1 John 2:24), or of abiding in eschatological life (2:17), now is used of doctrine: "he who abides in the doctrine. . . ." The christological doctrine that one must abide in is the orthodox confession that Jesus Christ has come in the flesh. The person who does not embrace that doctrine about the Son does not have valid belief in God either. The author contrasts this with the one who does abide in the doctrine, who has both.

Now comes the warning to have nothing to do with the purveyors of false doctrine (vv. 10–11). Contamination by association is to be avoided by not showing hospitality to the heretics or even greeting them. New Testament Christians, especially apostles, teachers, and leaders, traveled a great deal from one city to another, founding and visiting churches. Paul is the supreme example of this kind of itineracy, but he was more or less typical, not exceptional (cf. 1 Cor. 9:5–6). As they traveled, Christians relied a great deal on reciprocal hospitality, particularly the hospitality of more affluent Christians who owned houses and presided over households. (Ancient inns were often unsavory places!) This issue becomes even more important in 3 John (vv. 5–8). The prohibition of hospitality and even greeting is intended to keep the bearers of false doctrine out of the Elder's churches, thus preventing them from getting a foothold. In this context then, the NRSV's prohibition against welcoming, rather than simply greeting (RSV), such people is entirely appropriate. Greeting is apparently the equivalent of welcoming or receiving (v. 10). The note of warning is intended to put the church on notice that to tolerate the opponents is to offer them comfort and support and to bring oneself into danger. Far better to avoid them as well as their false teaching.

145

Interpreters note the close relation of 2 John to 1 John, particularly to the polemic against opponents and secessionists found there. Sometimes 2 John is said to be repetitive of that aspect of 1 John, and so it is. This is not, however, grounds for taking 2 John to be a spurious letter, that is, a letter in form only but actually not a real communication addressed to a specific audience and situation. In fact, it is difficult to imagine why, or for what purpose, a document like 2 John would have been composed if it were not a real letter. It adds nothing to 1 John except the prohibition against extending hospitality to, or even greeting, the antichrist opponents, and the warning to the readers not to jeopardize their own standing by doing so. Apparently the letter was written to emphasize the danger represented by the opponents, specifically the danger inherent in offering them any support or fellowship. It was they who broke fellowship in the first instance, and they must continue to be denied it. What occasioned such a warning to this Christian community we can no longer know. It is, of course, an implication of this view of 2 John as a genuine letter that it was composed after 1 John, which it seems in any case to presuppose. Just as 1 John would seem rather strange and obscure apart from the Gospel, so would 2 John apart from 1 John.

As for any distinctive Christian teaching in 2 John, there is virtually nothing that has not been said already in 1 John. As has already been observed, the old, not new, commandment of love (vv. 5–6) has already been discussed in 1 John (2:7–11; 3:11–18; 4:13–21), as have the separatists, the opponents, and their doctrine (2:18–19; 4:1–5). In pursuing either subject, it is better to start with 1 John and draw upon 2 John in support.

Rarely is 2 John prescribed in lectionaries as a text for preaching. It does not appear in any cycle of the Common Lectionary, probably for reasons similar to those just cited. What is treated here has already been said more thoroughly, if not better, in 1 John. John Calvin wrote commentaries on the Gospel and First Epistle but not on 2 and 3 John. Similarly, Luther lectured on 1 John but not on these very brief letters.

Perhaps the unique feature of this letter is best left unheeded, namely, the warning not to show hospitality or even friendliness to those who espouse false doctrine and do not walk in love. Shunning may still be practiced by the Amish, but it is not in good odor in modern society or modern churches. To be inhospitable and unfriendly is bad form. Incivility neither has, nor needs, defenders. In the face of it, normal human relations suffer. There is a sufficiency of bigotry and intolerance about, so that we do not need the Second Epistle to encourage it.

On the other hand, the Elder must be credited with a kind of seriousness that much so-called mainline Christianity seems to lack. We want to be thought of as liberal and tolerant above all things. The Elder's seriousness and stringency are scarcely congenial with a Christianity that wants to be accepted and accepting in a tolerant society whose mores set the standards for acceptable behavior even in the church. Christians with unyielding convictions are an inconvenience in modern society, as in ancient. Liberality and tolerance can mask not caring deeply or not taking crucial issues with utmost seriousness, or, to put matters differently, they can reveal a kind of failure of nerve, for which nothing matters deeply or seems really important. The Elder's unattractive intolerance attests his seriousness and his conviction that doctrine that undercuts Christian faith and conduct that undermines Christian community are not to be tolerated or condoned. We may be more liberal, civil, or tolerant, but are we as convinced of the necessity of proper Christian confession and genuine Christian community, or as appalled by its absence?

2 John 12–13
I Hope to See You:
A Traditional Epistolary Conclusion

The conclusion of the letter, in which the author expresses his hope to make a visit, is very much like that of 3 John 13–14, as well as reminiscent of Paul (Rom. 15:24; 1 Cor. 16:5–6; 2 Cor. 13:2). It is sometimes taken as an imitation of 3 John, a letter that deals with more specific and personal matters and is thus considered an original and authentic letter on which 2 John is based. In that case, 2 John is viewed as a brief tract cast in the form of a letter. As we have already observed, however, it then becomes a problem to explain the purpose of such a brief tract,

147

which adds nothing to what is already said in 1 John. As a letter, its obvious purpose is to warn the members of a congregation away from the opponents of the Elder.

The hope for a visit is quite natural and normal, and the fact that it is expressed in almost the same words as used in 3 John is not a compelling reason for thinking it was written by another author who was imitating the first letter's style. Word processors now produce letters with interchangeable parts. Epistolary conventions are fairly firmly fixed, whether in ancient times or modern. If the Elder wrote 2 John to one congregation and 3 John to Gaius, probably a member of a different congregation, it is not unlikely that he would have composed a similar concluding paragraph for both letters.

The questions of which was written first, from where they were written, and when they were written are really unanswerable. The tradition that connects the Johannine literature with Ephesus, a major Christian center, and puts the composition of these documents at the turn of the century, remains plausible. The Book of Revelation, which also belongs to the Johannine circle, was written in nearby Patmos. Conceivably the Johannine circle of churches, of which we find evidence in the letters, existed in and around the city of Ephesus, which after Rome and Alexandria was one of the great urban centers of the ancient Mediterranean world. The "children of your elect sister" (v. 13) are apparently the members of the church from which the Elder writes "to the Elect Lady and her children" (v. 1). As we have observed, the Elder's concern and care for his churches is very much like the Apostle Paul's. Apparently he stood in relation to these churches in very much the same position as did Paul to his.

Third John

3 John 1
The Beloved Gaius: An Urgent Letter

This is a personal letter from the Elder to Gaius (v. 1), one of two undoubtedly genuine personal letters from one person to another in the New Testament; the other is Paul's letter to Philemon. (The letters to Timothy and Titus, even if genuine letters, are much more official communications for the general guidance of the churches than personal letters of this sort.) Probably as Philemon gained a place in the New Testament because it was written by the Apostle Paul, so 3 John was eventually accepted by virtue of its association with John.

Following epistolary form, the Elder names himself first and then his addressee, Gaius. "Gaius" was a common name. Paul names a Gaius who is his host, probably in Corinth (Rom. 16:23), who is presumably the same Gaius of Corinth mentioned in 1 Corinthians 1:14. A Gaius turns up with Paul in Ephesus (Acts 19:29) and is identified there as a Macedonian; presumably he is not the same person as the Gaius of Derbe (a city in Asia Minor) mentioned a little farther along (Acts 20:4). Paul may well be dealing with three different persons of the same name. The Gaius of 3 John is likely another Gaius still. He is, however, linked, albeit remotely, with the Gaius of Romans 16:23, in that both would seem to be householders who could play host to other Christians (3 John 5–6). This fact has an important bearing upon the content and nature of 3 John, as we shall see. It is barely possible that 3 John is addressed to Gaius of Corinth in that city, but since no ancient tradition or other evidence connects 3 John, or any of the Johannine writings, with Corinth, this seems unlikely. Moreover, 3 John was written a generation after Romans. Probably 3 John originated in Asia, in the neighbor-

149

hood of Ephesus, as ancient tradition holds. Otherwise, there is no way we can trace its origin or destination.

While certainty about authorship is scarcely possible on the basis of so brief a document, tradition, as well as the use of typically Johannine language and themes (truth, love), are on the side of common authorship with 1 and 2 John. It is reasonable to suppose that 1 John was written first, and perhaps sent to several Johannine churches, and was followed by 2 and 3 John, which were written about specific matters to individual congregations.

With his address to the beloved Gaius, the Elder (cf. 2 John 1), strikes both a personal and a theological note. Again he expresses his own affection (and in exactly the same way as in the greeting of 2 John). At the same time he enunciates the now familiar Johannine theological theme of love and undergirds it by reference to truth. Truth, as we have seen, is a surrogate or synonym for Jesus Christ himself, so the basis of this loving relationship is immediately set forth: It is more than personal, but nevertheless personal also, and the Elder will appeal to that personal relationship.

3 John 2–4
A Prayer for the Beloved: More than a Conventional Form

While 3 John lacks a benediction (cf. 2 John 3), it contains the rudiments of an opening prayer or thanksgiving, similar to the Pauline thanksgivings (e.g., 1 Cor. 1:4–9) that were more or less conventional in ancient Hellenistic letters. The prayer fades out (vv. 3–4) as Paul's sometimes do (e.g., 1 Thess. 1:2–10) into ordinary discourse. It is quite conventional and might have appeared in almost any ancient letter. The statement that things are well with Gaius's soul (Greek: *psychē*) is also conventional and could be translated "with your life" or simply "with you." In the Johannine literature *psychē* is usually best translated "life." The language is not necessarily or specifically Christian at all, despite the connotation of "soul" in the history of Christian piety.

150

Again, verses 3–4 sound like 2 John 4 except that the Elder informs Gaius that some brethren have arrived and "testified to the truth" of his life (RSV). (Actually, the Greek reads only "to your truth"; the NRSV has "your faithfulness to the truth.") "Following the truth" is literally "walking in the truth," with all that connotes (as in 2 John 4, 6), in verses 3 and 4. That Christians report on each other, here quite positively, should not surprise us. We find the same practice reflected in Paul's letters. Sometimes the reports are positive (1 Thess. 1:6–8), but they may be troubling (1 Cor. 1:11). In any case, such reports back to an authoritative figure are quite analogous in Paul and John. The similar authoritative function of Paul and the Elder is sufficient to account for this, without our supposing that there is somehow a literary dependence of 3 John on one or more of the Pauline letters. The Elder obviously includes Gaius among his own children ("my children"), a familiar Johannine manner of speaking, but, interestingly enough, apart from 1 John 2:1 ("my little children"), this is the only occurrence of *"my* children" in the Johannine letters.

The Elder's greeting constitutes a full endorsement of Gaius and implies that he is trusted completely. No doubt this was the case, but the Elder's unreserved and wholehearted approbation is well calculated to insure the loyalty of Gaius, if ever there was any doubt. As will become apparent, the Elder wants to marshall his forces, those who are loyal to him, in the face of opposition in the church, a strategy that soon becomes evident in the letter (vv. 9–10).

3 John 5–8
Service to the Brethren: Christian Hospitality

The Elder praises Gaius for his hospitality to emissaries, who were likely representing the Elder himself. Although it is not said explicitly that Gaius offered them hospitality and thus was a householder ("home owner"), that was probably the case. Sending them on their journey (v. 6) implies that the guests had stayed at Gaius' house. It is noteworthy that the emissaries

151

include strangers (v. 5), eloquent testimony to the universality of the church, which is already a worldwide community binding together in faith in Jesus Christ and mutual love people who have never seen one another.

The emissaries have apparently reported Gaius's hospitality to the Elder ("before the church"), and this acceptance and love may be the concrete basis for the preceding praise of Gaius. (In fact, the testimony referred to in verses 6 and 3 may be the same; if so, this would confirm the supposition that the guests to whom Gaius had shown hospitality were the emissaries of the Elder.) The future tense ("You will do well to send them. . . .") apparently anticipates their future opportunities on the basis of their past performance. Otherwise, the future tense here does not jibe exactly with the fact that at least some of the brethren, having received support (or hospitality), have already reported back to the Elder. In any event, it is no great problem, and we are simply not told enough of the details of their travel to resolve it.

The people Gaius received were Christian missionaries, whose conduct is described succinctly by the Elder (v. 7). Because they do not accept support from those among whom they work, they deserve and need the help of other Christians. The RSV renders the *ethnikoi,* from whom the missionaries receive no support, "heathen"; the NRSV has "non-believers." In view of the missionary practice that is in view (below), the latter translation seems preferable.

Once again Paul's letters and missionary practice may shed light on this letter. Unlike peripatetic philosophers, with whom they might have been compared, these Christian missionaries did not live off those they sought to attract by their preaching. Paul reminds the Corinthians of his own previous practice in this regard (1 Cor. 9:3–7, 12; 2 Cor. 11:7–11). Moreover, he makes clear that other churches have supported his work so that he would not initially have to accept support from those for whom he was working as missionary (Phil. 4:15–17).

The Elder's statement that they have been "accepting no support from non-believers" (NRSV) makes sense in the light of Paul's practice. There would have been no reason for the Christian missionaries to accept anything from the heathen (i.e., Gentiles or pagans) unless they were somehow in contact with them, presumably seeking to win them over. It is also possible that there is an implicit contrast with the practice of the Elder's opponents, the secessionists and heretics who "went out from us" (1 John 2:19) and to whom the world listens (1 John 4:5). In any event, by supporting the good people allied with the Elder, Gaius and company share in their work and become "fellow workers in the truth," that is, in the gospel of Jesus Christ. (Here the RSV's "fellow workers in the truth" seems preferable to the NRSV's "co-workers with the truth," which not only is less literal but introduces a synergism that rings strange in these letters.)

3 John 9–10
Diotrephes, Who Likes to Put Himself First: Early Church Politics

Diotrephes and the Elder were at odds. What was going on between them? Obviously the Elder has written to Gaius's church: The description of what Diotrephes has done (v. 9)—or failed to do—needs clarification. The RSV's translation, "does not acknowledge my authority" is quite possible and may be correct, but it is not the only possibility that the Greek text presents. It could be translated more literally "does not receive us," which might, however, amount to the same thing. Diotrephes does not receive the Elder in the sense of granting him his authority. But probably Diotrephes's refusal to extend hospitality is also in view (cf. v. 10). The description of Diotrephes as one who loves first place is telling and doubtless led the translators to follow the course they chose.

The Elder becomes specific at the point of complaining that Diotrephes slanders him, presumably in the church, and does not receive "the brethren" (NRSV: "friends"), presumably the Elder's emissaries (v. 10). (NRSV's "spreading false charges against us" is more idiomatic than RSV's "prating against me with evil words.") Moreover, he refuses to let anyone else in the church receive them on pain of expulsion. Here again it is a question of mutual hospitality among Christians. One cannot help but recall 2 John 10–11, the Elder's warning not to receive the heretic into one's house, lest one share his wicked work. Is the shoe now on the other foot? Diotrephes rejects the Elder's emissaries and considers those who show them hospitality to be

153

in league with them. If 2 and 3 John are by the same author, the measures recommended by the Elder in the one letter are being applied to him by Diotrephes in the other. Is it conceivable the letters are by different persons on opposite sides of the issue, and that 3 John represents the reaction of one Elder to measures instituted by the other? There was more than one elder in the ancient church and perhaps also in the Johannine school.

One problem with this tempting solution is that 3 John makes no mention of the doctrinal or theological controversy so prominent in 2 John. If we had 3 John only, we might think it concerned nothing more than a jurisdictional dispute between rival church authorities. Indeed, were there the sharp theological differences made explicit in 2 John, 3 John would probably have given more than a hint of them. The Elder would not have missed the opportunity to polemicize against Diotrephes if he believed his teaching was in error, or to defend himself. Yet he does neither. What is, of course, obvious is the sharp dispute over jurisdiction and authority.

The Elder's fundamental problem with Diotrephes is very likely captured in the RSV's (and NRSV's) interpretative translation in verse 9: ". . . does not acknowledge my [NRSV: "our"] authority" (Greek: ". . . does not receive us"). The failure to extend hospitality is then an outgrowth of this attitude. Obviously, Diotrephes acts, or threatens to act, as an authoritative church leader himself, indeed one with the power to exercise church discipline even to the point of excommunication. Now the point of the commendation of Gaius's hospitality to the emissaries of the Elder comes into clear focus. Gaius has apparently done what Diotrephes has refused to do and forbidden (vv. 5–6). Presumably Gaius and Diotrephes belong to the same church or are in close proximity to each other. All the more reason for the Elder to commend and encourage Gaius, who has evidently defied Diotrephes's authority. With the contemplated visit of the Elder to Gaius's (and Diotrephes's) church, the battle would be joined (v. 10; cf. vv. 13–14). Like the Apostle Paul (cf. 2 Cor. 13:1–4), the Elder expects that his presence will turn the tide in his favor. The future condition and future tense in verse 10 imply that the visit is still uncertain, yet the concluding statement (v. 13) indicates that the Elder actually intends to make it.

154

REFLECTION:
Authority and Church Office in the Johannine Letters

Because Diotrephes is said to like to put himself first and the Elder obviously believes such authority is rightly his own, the question of what specific authority or office either or both of them claimed has naturally arisen. As we have already observed, the Johannine letters do not mention any apostolic or ecclesiastical rank or office, except that the author refers to himself as "the Elder." Whether the title denotes an office, or simply means an older man who is obviously a leader, is a good question. The Book of Acts mentions elders, presumably as officers of the church, fairly frequently (Greek: *presbyteros;* Acts 11:30, 14:23; 15:2). They appear also in 1 Timothy, where the term sometimes seems to refer to older men and women (5:1-2), sometimes to church leaders (5:17, 19). Perhaps we find the same ambiguity of age or office in the Pauline Pastorals and the Johannine letters. In the Pastorals, however, we read of a council of elders (1 Tim. 4:14) and of elders who rule (5:17), so a church office is more clearly in view.

Although apostles and church officers such as bishops are mentioned even as early as Paul (on "bishop"—Greek: *episkopos*—see Phil. 1:1-2 as well as 1 Tim. 3:1-7), these titles do not appear in the Johannine letters, quite a remarkable omission in view of the apparent similarities of pastoral and authoritative function that we have already observed. The possibility that the Elder deliberately eschews the title "apostle" has, not surprisingly, been suggested. Perhaps he represents a different, and more primitive, conception of church authority based on some combination of spiritual endowment and original witness or eyewitness. In 1 John we observed how often the author appealed to the beginning, that is, to Jesus, and the authoritative witness to him. Given such a view of authority, does Diotrephes represent a different concept of church authority or only a rival claim? Diotrephes, it is said, is one "who likes to put himself first." The Greek term, here used in participial form, seems to mean just that but does not occur elsewhere in the

155

New Testament. Does it imply more than it says? Does Diotrephes claim or occupy the office of the monarchical bishop, standing perhaps in apostolic succession, in a form or manner analogous to what is found in the Pauline Pastorals? If so, the Elder would be resisting not only Diotrephes personally but a whole concept of authority or authoritative structure in the church.

Several decades ago Ernst Käsemann published in German a classic article entitled "Heretic and Witness" *(Ketzer und Zeuge)* in which he proposed that the Elder stood over against the orthodox Diotrephes, an emerging bishop, as the representative of a more primitive form of inspiration and authority. Moreover, the Elder's own theological position was subject to question. He had, in fact, been excommunicated by the orthodox Diotrephes because of his faintly heretical association with Gnosticism. In his commentary, Bultmann rightly judges this last proposal somewhat fanciful, although he agrees that Diotrephes may well have represented the advancing orthodoxy of church tradition and authority. Eduard Schweizer, in his excellent work *Church Order in the New Testament,* has argued that the Johannine letters embody a form of church life, and of ecclesiology, in which the work of the Spirit and the believer's direct relationship, through the Spirit, to Jesus precludes the development of church order and organizational structure. Thus he, in effect, agrees with Käsemann on the ecclesiology of the Johannine letters, as well as the Gospel, as contrasted with other later New Testament books such as the Pauline Pastorals. His assessment is thus amenable to Käsemann's thesis about Diotrephes and the Elder but does not require it.

On the other hand, the evidence afforded by our text is so slim that a case can actually be made for the reverse of Käsemann's proposal about the relationship of Diotrephes and the Elder. Long before Käsemann wrote, B. H. Streeter, in *The Primitive Church* (1929), had seen in Diotrephes a local, relatively minor monarchical bishop, but in the Elder one occupying "a position of almost patriarchal prestige" in his own and neighboring churches (p. 84). Thus, far from being a heretic and witness or representing a low-church ecclesiology, the Elder was, in effect, an archbishop. Moreover, Streeter holds "that the evolution of church order in the New Testament culminates in the Johannine writings" (p. 89). Given Schweizer's persuasive treatment of Johannine ecclesiology, I find Streeter's view problematic. Nevertheless, it remains one way of construing the silence of John, particularly if one believes it possible and feasible to view John in continuity with other New Testament books or traditions that speak more explicitly to the development of ecclesiology and church order.

We have a seminal and suggestive text, upon which more than one historical interpretation can be put and indeed made to fit. The most one can say with certainty is that in 3 John the jurisdictions or spheres and claims to authority of two rival church leaders collide with reverberations heard down the centuries of interpretation. Whether Diotrephes and the Elder represent a clash of concepts of authority or only of claims to authority is finally impossible to decide.

3 John 11–15
Beloved, Imitate Good: Concluding Exhortations

We have here four relatively unrelated concluding remarks: verses 11, 12, 13–14, and 15. Apparently, the nature and content of verses 13–14 and 15 determine their place in the letter. The general exhortation of verse 11 may subtly refer to the Elder and Diotrephes, encouraging Gaius to continue to follow him while rejecting Diotrephes. The dualistic quality of Johannine thought again becomes quite evident. Although the content of the letter pertains to practical matters and church politics, its occasional rhetorical flourishes are distinctly Johannine (vv. 1, 4, 11, 12).

Probably verse 12 commends the bearer of the letter, although Demetrius's function is not made explicit. He is evidently someone who needs the Elder's introduction to Gaius. Letters of recommendation were sometimes necessary in the early church, particularly in view of the extensive travels of some leaders (cf. 2 Cor. 3:1–3). As has already been noted, verses 13–14 anticipate the Elder's visit to the church, on which occasion he will deal further with Diotrephes. The final benediction of verse 15 ("Peace be to you") is typically Johannine (cf. John 20:19, 26) but has parallels also in other early Christian

157

writings (1 Peter 5:14; Eph. 6:23; Gal. 6:16). Paul's final blessing is typically "grace" rather than "peace" (e.g., 1 Cor. 16:23). Once again, however, we note elements of an epistolary style common among Christian letter writers, the first and most prominent of whom was Paul.

Yet John has its own distinctive touches, clearly evident, for example, in verse 12. The motifs of testimony and truth, so prominent in this verse, are characteristically Johannine. Again "the truth itself" would seem a veiled way of referring to Jesus (cf. v. 1). Most intriguing, however, is the Elder's own testimony or witness and his signature (NRSV): "and you know our testimony is true." It immediately recalls John 19:35 and 21:24 and the attestation of the witness (in all cases *martyria*) of the piercing of Jesus' side or of his ministry generally. The Elder's statement scarcely proves that he is the one who bore witness to Jesus himself, but it certainly indicates that he belongs to the tradition and Christian community that attached great importance to such a witness, and in which it had become a sort of byword or hallmark of identification.

The preacher or teacher who approaches 3 John in search of a distinctive or important Christian doctrine or a fertile or fruitful text for preaching will likely be disappointed. As our exegesis shows, we find here the literary remains, slim as they are, of an intrachurch dispute over jurisdiction and authority. What could be less exciting or relevant? As 2 John has urged the shunning of opponents, 3 John expresses the dismay of those shunned. If there is an obvious lesson, is it not that Christians should be nicer to each other? Probably we should be, although sometimes we may be too nice when important issues are at stake.

The importance of 3 John lies, however, not in what it directly teaches or whether it contains a message that will preach, but in the crucially important issue that it raises. The dispute between the Elder and Diotrephes, petty though it may at first appear, is finally not insignificant, for it concerns the question of authority, not viewed in the abstract (scripture, Spirit, church, episcopacy), but in a very concrete and specific instance. Who has the right to speak to others in the church in matters of discipline and doctrine in order to say definitively what is permissible or impermissible, truth or error? The issue of jurisdiction is meaningless unless it involves authority, as it

158

surely does in 3 John. Diotrephes, who likes to put himself first, exercises authority in the church to forbid the reception of some visitors and to threaten punishment of those who disobey his decree. What we are not told is what issue other than that of authority per se is involved here. Quite possibly there was such an issue, although if it were explicitly theological it is surprising that it is not suggested in the letter.

When the Elder says, "You know my testimony is true" (v. 12), he not only strikes a familiar note but refers obliquely to the ground and the guarantor of authority in the Johannine church. That is, he evokes the witness of the Beloved Disciple (cf. John 19:35; 21:24), who is the sure and well-attested link to the earthly, as well as to the risen, Jesus. Although he does not claim to be that Disciple, he clearly wishes to indicate where the source of his authority lies. Would Diotrephes have been able to call upon the same authority? We do not know, although if he too was a member of the broader circle of churches we call Johannine, he probably would have claimed the same authority.

The rival claims of Diotrephes and the Elder lead us to posit the existence within the Johannine churches or community of a teaching office claiming the authority of the Beloved Disciple, and ultimately of Jesus himself. In all probability that teaching office claims inspiration by the Spirit (cf. 1 John 4:13 and the various Johannine passages cited there). But John found it necessary to appeal again to origins—to Jesus ultimately—to ground his authority, as he does repeatedly in 1 John. The Gospel of John can be viewed as a similar appeal on a grander scale, but it is 1 John that so dramatically and emphatically makes this appeal explicit. This teaching office with its appeal to Jesus as well as to the Spirit was authenticated in and by the community ("*We* know . . ."). Nevertheless, in the very nature of the case the teaching office or authority distinguishes itself from the community while remaining a part of it. One could say, therefore, that the Johannine school distinguishes itself from the Johannine community as a whole. As we have continually observed, there are strong affinities with Paul, his apostolic authority and mission. The affinities seem more functional than terminological but are not for that reason less important.

Paul insists on the importance of the apostolic role and office to which he lays claim. Curiously enough, the term "apostle" appears rarely in the Johannine literature, even when Revelation is included (once in the Gospel, three times in

159

Revelation, but not at all in the letters). It would be difficult, however, to defend the proposition that the Johannine letters represent a nonapostolic church. To all appearances, the Beloved Disciple, the Fourth Evangelist, and the Elder fulfill distinctly apostolic roles, whether they be one person or, as I think more likely, two or even three, spread over at least two generations. They were sent out with a commission. There is a sense in which they and the problems besetting the Johannine community demonstrate the indispensability of the principle of apostolicity, which grew up as a way of warranting or legitimating authority in the church.

In fact, we find here a microcosm of the situation of the early church as the problem of authority unfolds. There is the claim to have been a witness to Jesus; there is the inspiration of the Holy Spirit; there are figures within the community claiming authority; there are written documents—first a Gospel, then letters, at some point the Book of Revelation—all claiming either directly or indirectly to convey an authoritative message to the community. All intend to make good on the claim to convey the revelation of Jesus Christ, embodied in such epigrammatic sayings as: "That which was from the beginning, which we have heard, which we have seen with our eyes, which we have looked upon and touched with our hands, concerning the word of life." Jesus was a real, historic figure. To speak authentically of a revelation of God through him meant to invoke the authority of an historic witness, that is, of apostles, those sent out by him. In ways we can no longer fathom historically, the author of these letters was such an emissary.

BIBLIOGRAPHY

1. For further study of the Johannine letters

BROOKE, A. E. *A Critical and Exegetical Commentary on the Johannine Epistles.* INTERNATIONAL CRITICAL COMMENTARY. Edinburgh: T. & T. Clark, 1912.

BROWN, RAYMOND E. *The Community of the Beloved Disciple.* New York: Paulist Press, 1979.

―――. *The Epistles of John.* ANCHOR BIBLE 30. Garden City, N.Y.: Doubleday, 1982.

BULTMANN, RUDOLF. *The Johannine Epistles.* Translated by A. Philip O'Hara, Lane C. McGaughy, and Robert W. Frank. HERMENEIA. Philadelphia: Fortress Press, 1973.

DODD, C. H. *The Johannine Epistles.* MOFFATT NEW TESTAMENT COMMENTARY. London: Hodder & Stoughton, 1946.

GRAYSTON, KENNETH. *The Johannine Epistles.* NEW CENTURY BIBLE. Grand Rapids: Wm. B. Eerdmans Publishing Co., 1984.

HOULDEN, J. L. *A Commentary on the Johannine Epistles.* HARPER'S NEW TESTAMENT COMMENTARIES. New York: Harper & Row, 1973.

LIEU, JUDITH. *The Second and Third Epistles of John.* STUDIES OF THE NEW TESTAMENT AND ITS WORLD. Edinburgh: T. & T. Clark, 1986.

―――. *The Theology of the Johannine Epistles.* NEW TESTAMENT THEOLOGY. Cambridge: Cambridge University Press, 1991.

MARSHALL, I. H. *The Epistles of John.* NEW INTERNATIONAL COMMENTARY ON THE NEW TESTAMENT. Grand Rapids: Wm. B. Eerdmans Publishing Co., 1978.

PERKINS, PHEME. *The Johannine Epistles.* NEW TESTAMENT MESSAGE 21. Wilmington, Del.: Michael Glazier, 1979.

SMALLEY, STEPHEN S. *1, 2, 3 John.* WORD BIBLICAL COMMENTARY 51. Waco, Tex.: Word, 1984.

WILDER, AMOS. "Introduction and Exegesis of the First, Second, and Third Epistles of John." In *The Interpreter's Bible,* vol. 12, pp. 207–313. Nashville: Abingdon Press, 1957.

2. Other literature cited

ABBOTT, A. E. *Johannine Vocabulary: A Comparison of the Words of the Fourth Gospel with Those of the Three.* London: Black, 1905.

The Apostolic Fathers. Translated by Kirsopp Lake. 2 vols. LOEB CLASSICAL LIBRARY. Cambridge, Mass.: Harvard University Press, 1912, 1913.

BROWN, RAYMOND E. *The Gospel According to John.* ANCHOR BIBLE 29 and 29A. Garden City, N.Y.: Doubleday, 1966, 1970.

BULTMANN, RUDOLF. *The Gospel of John: A Commentary.* Translated by G. R. Beasley-Murray, R. W. N. Hoare, and J. K. Riches. Philadelphia: Westminster Press, 1971.

CALVIN, JOHN. "The First Epistle of John." In *The Gospel According to John and the First Epistle of John.* Translated by T. H. L. Parker. Grand Rapids: Wm. B. Eerdmans Publishing Co., 1961.

CHARLESWORTH, JAMES H., ed. *John and the Dead Sea Scrolls.* New York: Crossroad, 1990. See pp. 76–106 for Charlesworth's article "A Critical Comparison of the Dualism in 1QS 3:13—4:26 and the 'Dualism' Contained in the Gospel of John," originally published in *New Testament Studies* 15 (1968–69):389–418.

The Common Lectionary: The Lectionary Proposed by the Consultation on Common Texts. New York: Church Hymnal Corp., 1983. Also Peter C. Bower, editor. *A Handbook for The Common Lectionary.* Philadelphia: Geneva Press, 1987.

CONZELMANN, HANS. "Was von Anfang war." In *Neutestamentliche Studien für Rudolf Bultmann.* BEIHEFTE ZUR ZEITSCHRIFT FÜR DIE NEUTESTAMENTLICHE WISSENSCHAFT 21, pp. 194–201. Berlin: Töpelmann, 1954.

CULPEPPER, R. ALAN. *The Johannine School: An Evaluation of the Johannine School Hypothesis Based on an Investigation of the Nature of Ancient Schools.* SOCIETY OF BIBLICAL LITERATURE DISSERTATION SERIES 26. Missoula, Mont.: Scholars Press, 1975.

EUSEBIUS. *The Ecclesiastical History.* Translated by Kirsopp Lake, J. E. L. Oulton, and H. J. Lawlor. 2 vols. LOEB CLASSI-

CAL LIBRARY. Cambridge, Mass.: Harvard University Press, 1926, 1932.

IRENAEUS. "Irenaeus Against Heresies." In *The Ante-Nicene Fathers: Translations of the Writings of the Fathers Down to A.D. 325.* Edited by A. Roberts and J. Donaldson. Revised by A. C. Cone. Vol. I, pp. 315–567. Grand Rapids: Wm. B. Eerdmans Publishing Co., 1981. (This edition was originally published in 1885.)

JUSTIN MARTYR. "The First Apology of Justin." In *The Ante-Nicene Fathers: Translations of the Writings of the Fathers Down to A.D. 325.* Edited by A. Roberts and J. Donaldson. Revised by A. C. Cone. Vol. I, pp. 163–187. Grand Rapids: Wm. B. Eerdmans Publishing Co., 1981. (This edition was originally published in 1885.)

KÄSEMANN, ERNST. "Ketzer und Zeuge: Zum johanneischen Verfasser-problem." In *Zeitschrift für Theologie und Kirche* 48 (1951): 292–311.

———. *The Testament of Jesus: A Study of the Gospel of John in the Light of Chapter 17.* Translated by Gerhard Krodel. Philadelphia: Fortress Press, 1968.

KITTEL, GERHARD, AND GERHARD FRIEDRICH, eds. *Theological Dictionary of the New Testament.* Translated by Geoffrey W. Bromiley. 10 vols. Grand Rapids: Wm. B. Eerdmans Publishing Co., 1964–1976.

———. *Theological Dictionary of the New Testament: Abridged in One Volume.* Edited and abridged by Geoffrey W. Bromiley. Grand Rapids: Wm. B. Eerdmans Publishing Co., 1985.

KÜMMEL, WERNER-GEORG. *Introduction to the New Testament.* Translated by Howard Clark Kee. Nashville: Abingdon Press, 1975.

LUTHER, MARTIN. *Lectures on the First Epistle of John.* In *Luther's Works: The Catholic Epistles.* Vol. 30. Edited by Jaroslav Pelikan and Walter A. Hansen. St. Louis: Concordia, 1967.

MARTYN, J. LOUIS. *History and Theology in the Fourth Gospel.* Rev. ed. Nashville: Abingdon Press, 1979.

SCHNACKENBURG, RUDOLF. *Die Johannesbriefe.* HERDERS THEOLOGISCHER KOMMENTAR ZUM NEUEN TESTAMENT III, 3. 7th edition. Freiburg: Herder, 1984.

SCHWEIZER, EDUARD. *Church Order in the New Testa-*

163

ment. Translated by Frank Clarke. STUDIES IN BIBLICAL THEOLOGY 32. London: SCM, 1961.

SLOYAN, GERARD S. *John.* INTERPRETATION: A BIBLE COMMENTARY FOR TEACHING AND PREACHING. Atlanta: John Knox Press, 1988.

SMITH, D. MOODY. *Johannine Christianity: Essays on Its Setting, Sources, and Theology.* Columbia, S.C.: University of South Carolina Press, 1984.

STRECKER, GEORG. *Die Johannesbriefe.* KRITISCH-EXEGETISCHER KOMMENTAR ÜBER DAS NEUE TESTAMENT 14. Göttingen: Vandenhoeck & Ruprecht, 1989.

STREETER, B. H. *The Primitive Church.* New York: Macmillan Co., 1929.

WESLEY, JOHN. *Standard Sermons.* Edited by Edward H. Sugden. 2 vols. London: Epworth Press, 1921.

———. *Explanatory Notes upon the New Testament.* London: Epworth Press, 1952.